THE ONLY WAY WAS UP

Gertrude A. White

**With an introduction by
Sally White and an
Appendix by Sylvia White.**

ISIS

LARGE PRINT

Oxford

Copyright © Sally and Sylvia White, 2006

First published in Great Britain 2006
by
Isis Publishing Ltd.

Published in Large Print 2006 by ISIS Publishing Ltd.,
7 Centremead, Osney Mead, Oxford OX2 0ES
by arrangement with
the Author

British Library Cataloguing in Publication Data
White, Gertrude A.
      The only way was up. – Large print ed.
      (Isis reminiscence series)
      1. White, Gertrude A.
      2. Large type books
      3. Great Britain – Social conditions – 20th century
      4. Great Britain – History – Edward VII, 1901–1910
      5. Great Britain – History – George V, 1910–1936
      I. Title
      941'.082'092

      ISBN–10 0–7531–9394–9 (hb)
      ISBN–13 978–0–7531–9394–5 (hb)
      ISBN 978–0–7531–9395–2 (pb)

Printed and bound in Great Britain by
T. J. International Ltd., Padstow, Cornwall

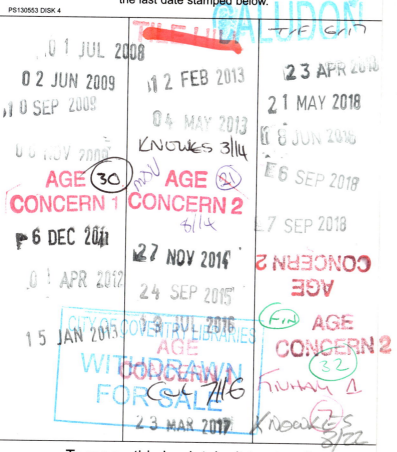

Introduction
by Sally White

Gertrude White was my paternal grandmother, Granny. She was not an easy person to get to know, let alone to love. She found it hard to love anyone apart from my father and, for a while, my elder brother, but he failed to reciprocate her feelings. She was, however, my only surviving grandmother and I wanted her love. It always seemed that simply by being female I was a disappointment to her. When I did not leave school at the earliest opportunity and talked of my wish to go to university she accused me of sponging off my father. One memorable year she gave my brother a useful cheque for Christmas while I received a pair of frumpish underpants. We were certainly not close. A couple of years before she died I was living abroad and we exchanged letters from time to time. I remember being ridiculously pleased when she wrote that at least I worked hard for what I wanted. This felt like high praise indeed. After she died I received a cheque from her executors and cried. I had wanted a grandmother who loved me and behaved like other people's Grannies rather than money after her death. I had no idea why she was so determined to keep the world at bay.

A few years ago I started to collect information about my family and my father gave me a manuscript written by Granny before she died that had come to him after his sister too was dead. Granny was born in 1897 and the manuscript told her story up to 1915. As I read it I was overwhelmed with sadness and incredulity. We had all known that Granny had been poor as a child but had had no inkling of the loveless penury in which she had existed. After all, everything about her later life was the epitome of middle class respectability. How could my grandmother have been in a workhouse? So much suddenly made sense and I felt terrible that none of us had known the depth of her suffering in her lifetime. I understood how desperately she had strived for, attained and clung on to the kind of middle class respectability she had craved when young.

I was also stunned at the quality of the writing. Granny's descriptive writing is wonderful and she clearly had the heightened clarity of memory which seems to afflict some people who have suffered deeply so that they do not just remember, they relive their experiences as vividly as when they experienced them for the first time. Because of this she managed to write in a way that pulls a reader in and entices him or her to read on, savouring the depth of her descriptions. She also wrote unflinchingly about subjects that many writers shy away from. She presents them unsentimentally but her pain is none the less tangible.

Some people who suffer later devote huge energy to trying to stop other people from suffering in the same way. Others seem to want other people to endure equal or worse hardships to those they have survived. Granny was in the latter group and did nothing to make the lives of people around her easy. Much of Granny's character shows in her writing, an arrogance about her talents, a sense of superiority which showed itself even as she began her climb to respectability, a wilful naivety and a lack of empathy with other people, but when you read her story it is hard not to empathise with and understand her.

Having read the manuscript I went and visited many of the places she described and found that I could identify them easily even eighty years or so later. It was a very moving journey and one I shared with my mother who had urged Granny to write about her life and to whom, in her later years, in spite of huge mutual antipathy Granny had told bits of the story.

The manuscript ends abruptly in 1915. She clearly meant to continue writing but never did. Who was the manuscript written for? At times I feel it was definitely written for an audience. I am also aware that my mother says that it was something Granny needed to do for herself. She had nobody of her generation with whom she could reminisce at all. Neither of her children showed much interest in her past. There is an irony in fact that I am the one who has transcribed and edited her text, coming to an understanding of her that I never managed in her lifetime, and that it is my mother, the daughter-in-law she disliked, who has written a warm appendix summarising her life after the end of the manuscript. It is a story that needs to be shared.

CHAPTER ONE

All my life I have had the itch to write. Again and again in the midst of my busy existence after my head had been teeming with sentences for days I have sat and scribbled guiltily for an hour or so, and as I used to say to myself, "got it out of my system", only to tear up later what I had written. I wrote poetry pretty consistently too, mostly sonnets or short verse in pencil between washing up and cooking meals, and frequently fished pieces of soggy paper out of my apron pockets in the washing tub. Now I am old I find quiet amusement at the attitude people take towards me. For years women have said, "Well, of course its different for you. You've been educated, and don't know what it's like to be hard up."

In reading biographies, where writers go back to their childhood I am astonished at the length of their memories. They can repeat, verbatim, conversations overheard when they were almost babies, and describe sunsets and scenes and buildings in detail which they saw when they were toddlers. I certainly can't do that. Perhaps it is because my childhood was so mixed up.

My first recollections come through smells. The smell of wet roses recalls to me the sense of being a small thing in a miraculous cave of scent and colour, which I realise was me crawling under a flower stall in an East End street market. The scent of bad oranges, the treasure trove of rotten fruit thrown under the fruit stalls, and a tub of pig swill at the farm at Weston when I was twelve made me again a tiny thing in a long, long queue in the courtyard of a huge building, holding a basin. And into the multitudinous basins someone was ladling a conglomeration of leavings which smelt just like this swill, very wholesome, I have no doubt, and very welcome to hungry ones. I passed a few years ago, a house which had that morning been burned down, and the air was full of the smell of wet, burnt wood, and I was suddenly filled with terror and desolation. I was again a small atom wailing in a crowd, eyes stinging with smoke watching the glare of flames and listening to the crackle of burning wood that meant the destruction of home. I had been told this had happened in our past, but had no actual recollection of it. Carbolic disinfectant brings cold, long corridors, brown tiled walls and hard, hard nurses with crackly starched aprons. The smell of bread and milk before it is sweetened recalls a long, bare room with a single scrubbed table, and a row of quiet, still old women with little tight, white bonnets on their heads, and complete silence. I have to put salt in the milk to get the picture properly.

My father was a Welshman who when young was happily married, with two tiny boys. His wife died on the birth of a third which also died. His wife's sister took the boys and brought them up; and very well too.

They have been most respected members of their town council, and their own sons are following in their steps. I saw one of them on television not long ago. Father was crazy with grief, and when the first Boer War came he joined the army. Alone in London a year later he met my mother and they were married two weeks later. She was a fine looking girl, but a cockney of cockneys, a coarse East Ender, a slut with no idea of home-making. He expected a neat, quiet housewife like his first wife, but she, who had been brought up in a slum, and thought music halls and street dancing and pubs — not that she was ever a heavy drinker — the nearest thing to heaven, was no good to him at all nor he to her. I don't think love ever came into it. Very soon they hated each other and he was drinking heavily and losing his jobs and knocking her about, and they went as low, I think, as was humanly possible. A frequent nightmare I had for years was the sound of shrieking voices and smashing crockery and blows, growing louder and louder till I woke with the sound of the banging of my own heart.

They had seven children under these conditions. First Jessie, then Tommy (who was blind and died as a tiny boy), Florrie who was an epileptic, then Dorothy, one of the loveliest children imaginable, then Edith, then me and then a stillborn baby who was the result of my father coming home before going overseas in the second Boer War. My mother had to work hard to keep us all. She fought hard in her way for us, but had the lowest possible standards. We were filthy and verminous, and her routine when we went to bed was to sit and scrape along the seams of our discarded garments with her fingernail to loosen the lice that she cracked between her thumbnails. I recall the fact of louse-hunting and the look of the flat grey things with a spot of colour in the middle which I realised years afterwards was a spot of human blood. I can remember once biting one to see if it tasted good, but it was only gritty.

We can't have had anything much in the way of furniture. My one dim vision of a room is a bedroom, absolutely bare except for a bed made up on the floor. We girls were all there, two at the top and two at the bottom, and I remember a loud rumbly noise that terrified me, which the others said was the Scotch Express, so we must have then been somewhere near one of the main railway lines. I was terrified of most things then, and it took me a long time to grow out of my fears. There were gratings in the pavements under which writhing things groped for your feet to pull you down. There was a chant about "Two white ghosties, sitting on two white posties, Gotcher!" — this last word, uttered with blood-curdling menace accompanied by crooked fingers waved in my face, would send me into sobbing paroxysms of terror. And there was a place called "Saffron 'ill" where Italians lived and they ate little girls. They lived down below where a road went under a bridge and there were steps leading down. It was great fun to the others and their mates to walk slowly over the bridge shouting insults to the people below, then run as they neared the steps, but I couldn't run as fast as the others, and only escaped being eaten alive by the nearest inch. I was what was called a sniveller, and the number of times I had my head clumped to make me stop snivelling was nobody's business. I spent a great deal of time in hospital, too, to judge from my mother's reminiscences later on.

Children in slum parts went to school early then, and my sisters went before they were four. They were desperately unhappy, at least Jessie and Dorothy were. They had to sit away from the other children because they were dirty, and were taunted with this all the time. Once a teacher brought Dorothy some clothes, a pretty brown velvet frock among other things, but she didn't repeat the experiment, because they were soon as ragged and dirty as the others. I suppose Dorothy was about seven then and a very bright child.

From what I have heard, Mother was the chief breadwinner all these years. At different times she took in washing, had a fruit stall in a fruit market and a greengrocer's shop. We had various uncles and at one time she had a young man working for her, and he is my other early memory. I see myself sitting on the bare floor of an empty room facing him, so near I could only see he had uncovered a part of his body and he was stroking it with my hand. Nothing else so I presume there was nothing else. I think our one fairly prosperous period came before this, when Mother had started a hand laundry, and did exceedingly well. She was a very good businesswoman, a hard worker, and employed several Irish washerwomen, and knew how to manage them and drive them. This must have been when I was about two, one of our innumerable moves when my

5

father was not in the army, and this was the place that was burned down. I have a store of Irish folk songs and music-hall songs, which I must have learned as I sat on the floor while these women sang as they worked. My mother had a lovely singing voice, though of course it had a cockney twang, and my father, I am told, a magnificent baritone.

Florrie, the epileptic, was passionately devoted to me, the baby, but as she grew, her malady became worse. She could not go to school, and I expect my mother very cheerfully left me to be minded by her, but she was not safe, and when thwarted, would attack me, the thing she loved. I have three scars even now, one on my head from when she threw me down on the stones and two on my hands, where she bit me in her frenzy. She was taken into a home, poor child, and never had freedom again.

It must have been soon after the stillborn baby that Mother left us. Father was still in the Army. Jessie was about eleven. She was a brilliantly clever, proud child, who loved my father and detested my mother — she had her capacity for hating. She loathed we younger ones, and never came home until night time if she could help it, when of course, her life was made very hard for her. She was awarded a scholarship at school, and her headmistress was very good to her, backing her up when my mother tried to make her leave, helping her with clothes and other things. As I have no personal knowledge of her as a child at all it is difficult for me to get her early life in perspective, but it must have been devilish. I'm told Mother would go round to the school

6

and create a scene, and try to drag the child away. I don't wonder she grew up to be hard and bitter where we were all concerned.

Doff, then about eight, was soft and sweet and pretty, and the one Mother really loved, but though she was favoured, life was no easier for her. Her mission in life, then, was to look after Dith, which took some doing, for she was a holy terror from the beginning. Like Jessie she hated Mother when a tiny thing and always afterwards, but more than all, she hated little, snivelling me. Whenever she could hurt me, either herself, or through others, she did, but Doff mothered her and loved her and protected her. I was just a thorough nuisance.

So, one night, three filthy, ragged, little girls, of 4, 6 and 8 were found crying on the steps of a London institution. I don't know which one. Mother had left us at a certain point, told Doff where to go, with instructions to say we were lost. She went away, leaving Jessie on the streets. Her headmistress must have helped her, for she made good, but at what a cost! And now I do have faint recollections, of several different places. I remember carbolic, and of crying bitterly in a huge, stinging bath and of someone saying I was sweet and of being scratched by Dith in consequence. And I remember sitting in a chair, all clean with my hair washed, and seeing Doff on her knees, in a big apron, scrubbing the floor because "she was a big girl". And of crying again, because they wouldn't talk to me because I was a "favourite". There was something about "finding our parish" and we were moved about quite a lot. I think it took them a long time to find out about us and our parents. The old women and the salted bread and milk come in somewhere here, but my first real memory is when I was about six, and was sent to a place called "The Downs" at Sutton. I was supposed to have ringworm, and remember being in a large room, it must have been a reception centre, with quite a lot of other children and grown-ups sitting on seats all around the walls.

Up to now I knew nothing of love and tenderness, and watched with amazement two nuns, who brought in a girl of about ten — she seemed very big to me, and beautiful. I, of course, was wearing institution dress, but she had dainty clothes, and long gleaming hair round her shoulders; but she was weeping, and the nuns were weeping, and caressing her and comforting her and assuring her of their love, and how she would soon be back with them again, and they would visit her every week — and I remember this as the first time that a dreadful wave of desolation swept over me, a feeling that was to visit me so many times over the next decade. I did not understand the love, but I longed for it with every scrap of my being.

The Downs really was a terrible place, utterly inhuman with bare walls, hard forms and scrubbed board floors, and starched aprons and hard faces and harder hands that boxed my ears if I cried or if I laughed — yes, in a hospital ward, with another child next to me I laughed out loud, and the nurse said, "I'll give you something to make you laugh the other side of your face," and she did. I remember the bewilderment

8

so well, and I cried all right. I can feel the soaking wet pillow now.

Each morning we stood in long rows in a kind of surgery ward, where a sister sat at the end of each row; a table was at her side with a basin full of instruments on it, to "treat" our heads. Absolute silence was the rule, and woe betide anyone who broke it. When I reached the sister I was pushed down and my head was held between her knees as in a vice, while she prodded my head with something sharp "for roots". I should have said that after the reception centre our heads were shaved, and we wore little white cotton bonnets. Nothing was ever explained to us, we were not soothed; I was full of terror at what was being done, and was a nuisance as I frequently fainted while on my knees. When this was discovered I was hauled to my feet by the scruff of my neck and dumped on a chair and brought back by the simple expedient of slapping my cheeks. I cannot remember one kind nurse, or doctor, or dentist: to them, I think, we were a job they had to do to get money, but not flesh and blood like their own children or relations. We had our teeth attended to, or pulled out, without any attempt at comfort and were most of us terrified and cried all the time.

By now, of course, I was getting to be a "big girl", and old enough to do jobs. I was nearly six. In pairs, we each made a certain number of beds each morning before surgery, and did a lot of folding up, but I can't remember what we folded, and we laid tables for meals, but everything had to done in silence — and how can you expect little girls not to talk. Two nurses would be sitting talking as we did our tasks, watching for the whispered word, or the smile that would show we were sharing something, and wham, down would come their heavy hands. Or they would have a gramophone playing. I remember once it was "Two Little Girls in Blue", and I was found to be humming the tune, and my ears were boxed and harsh voices shouted at me. Yet these women were poor class women, not trained nurses. Women you would have expected to have some sympathy for children in our position, but no, their theme was "who did we think we were, beggarly brats, they'd have to teach us to mind our places".

One task gave me a great deal of wretchedness. I, being a big girl, was given a small boy to "mind". His name was Freddie, but I have no recollection of him at all, and do not know his age. I don't suppose I was a particularly dependable child, but Freddie had a weakness for dirtying his knickers, and each time he did it I was the whipping boy. I also had to change his clothes and wash him down, and then be cuffed because I hadn't done it properly. He was a grizzler, too, and we kept each other company. I also had to clean a certain number of boots each day.

We didn't have our own personal sets of clothing. I can only remember the dresses and coats; they were kept on shelves according to ages, and we lined up in the passage outside the room, filed in, were given the garments that ought to fit our age and filed out again. Unfortunately, even institution children don't all come in the same size. I came of a tall family, was tall for my age, big-boned and not well covered. After dragging on the garment planned for a normal six-year old I was liable to be seen by an overlord, thumped and sent back for a better fit, when I would be given something about two sizes larger, which hung around me in folds. This dressing up was for our church-going. The clothes, on looking back, seem to me to have been good quality and warm, but had nothing in common with what children outside were wearing. The dresses, I remember, were striped and very long, the coats navy blue, also long and plain, and we wore small blue bonnets, like the ones the old ladies in the workhouse had worn, but what I felt and have never forgotten, was the soulless anonymity of the clothes. We wore them to go to church, took them off when we came in, they were taken away and put back, and anyone else might have them next time. The same method applied with boots and we wore thick, coarse, black stockings.

This churchgoing was to me a dread. We lined up, filed through the gates, and dragged along in a long crocodile in the gutter — not on the pavement. That was for the fortunate people outside, the young of which ran along beside us with catcalls and rude remarks, among which "workhouse kids" was by no means the worst. These occasions were the first on which I felt fierce resentment surge up inside me instead of the "grizzling" that the treatment inside the institution called forth. I remember walking along with my chin in the air, and a burning, choking pride battling with shame at my position, and I could have battered my fists in the faces of those jeering, horrible children. And I didn't like the silent, watching women any better, either. In church we sat in rows altogether at one side, but I have no recollection of anything that went on, only the dreadful walk back again.

I dimly remember a Christmas at this time. We were lined up, and had to tell the person in charge of what we wanted "Santa Claus" to bring us. I said, "a dollie, of my own" and was called a baby, but when the time came, and some smiling strangers were emptying the tree which I very dimly remember, instead of the cuddly dollie which I could dress and undress, I was given a small sailor boy doll, with clothes which would not take on or off. I hugged it half-heartedly because it was my own, but the toys were all taken from us after the ceremony and I only saw the doll once again. I was told a great girl like me didn't need dolls, but anyhow we none of us had any personal possessions. There was a so-called playroom, with cupboards into which these toys were put, and theoretically we played with them, but I honestly cannot remember ever doing so freely. We sat around the walls with our arms folded. Also here, apart from the church going, I cannot remember ever going outside the building for a walk, or any other purpose. I presume that in the afternoons, after the dreadful surgery was over, we went to school, but have no recollection of it at all.

CHAPTER
TWO

Then, somehow, I was moved, and found myself at a place called Mitcham, and it was to be wonderful because Dorothy was there. We were allowed to meet on my arrival, but she was happy there, and I think felt I would be a nuisance to her. However, she was a senior of eleven, and I not yet seven. I do not think we met again, though I think I saw her from a distance several times, and worshipped from afar. Here was a happier life altogether. I remember the vast dining room with plates full of thick bread and butter and jam on Sundays, and a "living" kind of atmosphere, and also I went to school, and for the first time enjoyed myself. I have a confused sense of someone being pleased with me — though I honestly have not one good recollection of a nurse, I have no bad one of a teacher. I enjoyed the singing and chanting of poetry and tables, and it was here I first began to emerge from the mass, for I quickly became one of the quickest and brightest, and learned and loved learning. Here happened a real Christmas, the first I really knew anything about. For weeks we were learning songs at school to sing at the "entertainment", and I was in several small singing groups. All I remember of the great day is that the tables in the dining hall were full of unfamiliar food, of which, unfortunately, I could not eat much (I found for years that the plain food and short commons of my early years made me unable to cope with plenty), and afterwards, the "entertainment". I cannot remember our junior part at all, although apparently, I was in it, as I sang alone a song about "I'm a merry little Jap Jap" I expect I looked the part physically, being pale and sharp faced, with hair that was only just growing after the gruelling treatment at The Downs, and even then I sang like a bird, as I have done all my life.

It is a curious thing about Dorothy. Since our adult days we have been very close. I have always loved and yearned for her, but she was, I think, always afraid as a child to own me in case I was a nuisance, and she never praised me. I remember sharply, again and again, when I have done something for which I have been praised outside my home, the stony silence with which my eager reports have been treated by the others, and the hostility and real unkindness with which Edith distorted all my efforts. There never was a child more grovelling to please her family, whose efforts met with less success.

That by the way. After the juniors, the highlight — a pantomime by the seniors, *Ali Baba and the Forty Thieves*. It was fairyland. It must have been well done, I think, and the music was quite good — for years I could sing almost all the songs. I had the words and music by heart, but have always been the same. When I first saw and heard the Gilbert and Sullivan Operas when I was eighteen, my first music except *The*

Messiah, I knew all the solo tunes the next morning, and sat down and wrote down all the words. But this was the first show of any kind I had seen, and one side of me knew the gorgeous creatures on the stage, in bright raiment and bathed in glowing light, were the big boys and girls of the senior side — wasn't Dorothy singing in the chorus? It really was a gallant young Gaynum singing to his beautiful Morgiana, "Dear Morgiana, sweet Morgiana, here now I come from afar, Love's music bringing, plaintively singing, though I possess no guitar", and when the boiling oil was poured in the jars I actually heard the robbers sizzling, and was suitably elated at the triumph of poverty and love over riches and villainy.

Another highlight gleams out. Probably there was some exceptionally good weather the next spring or summer, for I remember we were taken for a walk to some fields or a common, to play. There were hillocks and long grass and yellow bushes and small purply stuff, prickly to the legs, and we were told to roll and jump. I know that it didn't come naturally, but I mooned about and rubbed my face in the warm springy green, and felt I was in heaven, yet was afraid to move about too much for fear of what might be round the corner. The unknown, then, was terrifying; though it surely couldn't have been worse than I had known.

A blank occurs now till one day I was told it was my birthday — the first one I had had, apparently, and my mother had brought me a pot of homemade blackberry jam. It was put by my plate each breakfast and teatime till it was empty. I don't suppose it lasted long under the circumstances. As far as I know it was the only present I had ever had, the only personal belonging, and was the occasion of breathless happiness. It didn't apparently occur to me to wonder how or when my mother brought the jam, but I worked it out later that she had come to take Dorothy away and I myself was removed some three months later. My mother had obtained a job as manageress of the laundry at Felsted School, in Essex. She had three women working under her, and a man in the engine room, and took Doff, then eleven and eight months, a pretty, slim, willowy girl, none too strong, as a junior worker, supposed to be fourteen. No birth certificates were required in those days. She had obtained a two-roomed cottage ten minutes walk away from the laundry, which was in the school grounds, and was all set for us to get together again. Edith joined us a month or two later.

CHAPTER
THREE

I don't remember being taken there, I just was there. To me the cottage and the place were paradise. One walked from the station through the village, past the delightful houses of the school, past the playing fields, past a few cottages to a green country road, thick with grey dust or mud, or ruts — according to the season — and in summer bordered with golden wheat red with poppies, high above our heads. One came to a stile on the left, which led through fields to the laundry, and then there on the right was the cottage or rather three cottages in one.

Mr and Mrs Hatley, clean, spare and uncompromising, lived in the first, with a neat, well-stocked garden down to the road, then the Stubbinses in the next, with three rooms between seven of them, then our two rooms with cupboard on the end. A rough old cobbled path lead up to our front door, and growing to the side of it a magnificent walnut tree, famous all over the village. There was a large garden full of old gooseberry bushes, raspberry canes, old apple trees and plum trees, a wild pear, and a bullace tree, which was laden each year with sharpish but delicious pinky-white fruit, the size of a tiny plum. A great wooden shed with a thatched roof, in imminent danger of falling down, was in the shade of the walnut tree. It had been lined patchily from time to time with wallpaper, and seemed as if only that held it together. It smelled of damp and dirt; fungus of all kinds sprouted out of its sides and floor, but we loved it, and it was, to me especially, anything I desired it to be, accordingly, as my imagination developed, a school, a palace, a shop, but never, never, a hospital! Being alone every day except Sunday as we were, we were free as air, and could bring to the shed any precious bits of rubbish we found, for people threw into the hedges and ditches all their broken and unwanted bits, even more than they do now. We had no refuse collections then. I know we had a broken armchair made of metal strips which let down as a single bed (we had to put a box under it to hold it up), and a collection of old boxes which could be anything we wanted, but we had to keep quiet about them or we should have had to chop them up for firewood.

There was a bay tree under our downstairs room window, and what had been a flower garden, and we each had a piece to cultivate as our own. As we grew older we had a great deal of happiness from this, and would bring home primroses and violets and anemones from the fields and woods, though the latter never took, and little pansies which we called "Betsies", and, when we had our Saturday halfpenny, would, at the proper season, buy a packet of cornflower seeds, or Love-Lies-Bleeding, a wonderful name, that, or candytuft, or blood red linums or nasturtiums. I proved to have green fingers, and mine generally did well, though I suspect I worked a little more digging the ground over than Dith did, but Dorothy would fuss around if hers did come up, and eventually "kill them with kindness". This, of course, was another manifestation of my essential wrongness, and they would sniff and say, "Oh, yours, they would be marvellous", and so they were to me.

When Mother took the cottage for a shilling a week she had no furniture and no possessions, except one article, "The Hamper". This was made of wicker, and about the size of a small cabin trunk. It contained all she had in the world, hers and our clothes, spare bedding, if any, and was always our chief item of furniture. It was in turn table, sideboard or extra chair. At first we had only boxes to sit on, but gradually rickety chairs and a table were acquired, and pictures from jumble sales, and crockery throw-outs.

The rest of our ground, where the fruit trees and bushes were, was out from the side, stretching along the road frontage, with a hedge of wild plum which was a mass of white bloom in spring. The grass grew head high in spring and summer, with hemlock and plum-puddings and vetch and the loveliest ladies' lace and beautiful plumed grasses, and the cleanness and fragrance used to go to my head, and I'd lie stretched in it, soaking in its warmth, watching the little red or brown hopping insects busily clambering up and down the stalks. I could never bear to hurt one of them, and would go to infinite pains to save them from harm, and glow with satisfaction when I thought I had helped one.

One of the apple trees bore a lovely large red striped apple which dripped with juice when bitten into, and another was a Russet; Mother called it "Harvest Apple", I don't suppose she knew its name, but it was a delicious eater. A great lover of English apples, I have never tasted sweeter than those two. We had to gather the windfalls to take indoors, and after inspection were allowed to eat the unkeepables, but the perfect ones were hoarded and doled out for treats. Fortunately the red one proved a poor keeper, and in time Mother learned to let us have one each a day while they lasted. But woe betide us if we ate one without permission.

There were two poor green apple trees which were used for cooking, but we found plenty of wild plums and pears in the grass — the trees were too spindly and tall for us to reach to pick them and when they fell they were ripe and sweet and squashy — sometimes with wasps or earwigs in them. Once a summer some man would come and scythe the grass, and that was the time for finding sweet hidden fruit. Nettles grew tall around the gooseberries and raspberry canes, but we used to pick them and take the basinful indoors. I think they were pretty poor fruit, but we were not choosy. We used to get scratched and torn and the nettles were very painful. Dith said all I had to do was to hold them firmly and pull them up, and like the innocent I was, I did it, to her very great amusement. I was told Dad had played this trick on her. At the bottom of the garden was a hedge, and we could get through into Heaven, of which more later.

As I have said, we had one room up and one down. The outer door led straight into the room, and the stairs went up from the far corner. The one little window overlooked the front garden where the bay tree was, and the path which led to the road. Another door led to the cupboard, which was the food store on the right hand, and coal cellar on the left, a very convenient, if dirty, combination. There was a great treasure in this cupboard, a tea plant, which was rooted under the shelves at the food end, and spread out and along the wall to the coal end. How it grew in this dark hole — for there was no window — I cannot imagine, or how it ever got there, but there it was, and grow it did, and was famous, like our walnut tree and our bay tree. We were quite outcasts, of course, being people no village could be proud of, yet it was funny how some very respectable old lady would just happen to see us in the garden and quite condescendingly ask us for a couple of bay leaves or a slip of the tea plant, which was very fragrant.

The small fireplace was in the wall on the right as one went in, the wall between us and the Stubbinses, and there we did the cooking, very smokily. We had no mats on the floor and no curtains for a while, but one great day Mother bought two yards of white muslin with red poppies on it, for 2s 3/4d a yard, and we tacked up a pair of curtains, and hung them up with tape and felt very grand. Upstairs we had a large bed and one chair. Dorothy slept in the bed with Mother, and for a year or so Dith and I slept together on a straw mattress on the floor. There was no water in the cottage and no sink. Every morning Dith and I carried a bucket each to the farm opposite, and drew the day's supply from the pump and carried it back, no small undertaking for two girls of eight and ten.

It was somewhere between my birthday in September — the blackberry jam one — and Christmas that I went home, and I was oh so happy, and I think I began to fill out and bloom almost straight away. I had never been used to love and care, so the absence of that didn't worry me as much as it would had I been used to it, and I discovered a terrific joy in home-making and housekeeping, which was just as well really, as the other three were, in the home, lazy and dirty and utterly without pride at all. Of course Mother and poor Dorothy were tired out when they came in after working from seven till six and at first Mother made a show of preparing a meal for us all, but she was a ghastly cook, and would dish up half raw bloaters which made me sick — I have never eaten a bloater since those days — and half raw rice and oatmeal, and any attempt at pastry at the weekend, though we ate it because we were hungry, was like lead. Dith was then and always a lazy, lying, little bully, who got out of all her share of the work by threatening me, and daring me to say anything about it.

We were supposed to get ourselves up in the morning, eat our bread and jam — we had a lot of rhubarb in the garden and Mother made jam with the minimum of sugar and boiling and it was just a runny, sour sort of mess, but doubtless wholesome — wash up for the four, not an arduous job as we hadn't much

22

crockery, go to the farm for the water, go over again with a jug for a pennyworth of skim milk — a quart jug full for a penny, and then sprint down the road, ten minutes journey, to school. As I don't suppose two small girls were very quick at tumbling out of bed — Dith never was, but I developed a terrible sort of conscience as I grew older, besides which we went to bed early, and had plenty of sleep — things had a way of not being done in the mornings except the water and milk, which had to be fetched then or go without. At dinnertime we had mostly bread and dripping and/or bread and treacle and did some of our jobs. Edith soon formed the habit of taking her dinner to school with her. She became friendly with some of the bigger, tougher girls who brought their food also, and they amused themselves very well in the dinnertime break. Curiously, though I suppose they had young sisters of their own, they joined with Dith in persecuting me whenever we met, and it was nothing for several of them to come into our garden with her, jeer at my efforts indoors, run over my little flowers, and go away laden with windfalls which she knew we were not supposed to have, jeering at my feeble remonstrances with threats of what would happen to me if I "told". And I never did; things were made uncomfortable enough for me as it was, without adding to it. Her unfriendliness extended into school life, and she never acknowledged me in the playground, or was my big sister in the usual sense of the word, except in protecting me if I was attacked by boys, when she came into the fray like a lion and they flew from her.

I don't remember any woman or child ever coming into the cottage. As a family we had no friends at all. I played with the Stubbinses in our garden whenever they and I were allowed, but mostly surreptitiously. Mr Stubbins was a worker for the farmer who owned our cottages and his wife was a fat blowsy woman. There were several children who seemed grown up to me, then Annie, about eleven, Emily, a little younger than me, and little Jackie, about three. He was a large-headed, spindly legged little boy with a huge "dummy" always in his mouth; he used to cry a lot and run along the garden path tugging at his mother's skirt and crying out for "tittie", when she would pick him up and suckle him. She did wean him somewhere about this time, and he used to cry most pitifully. My mother always talked to us most slightingly about them as "yokels", and would most pointedly avoid even passing the time of day with them in the garden, and call me away from the old fence if the children were there, and quite a bad feeling grew up, but I should say they did infinitely better than we did. They must have been quite as poor, but the children were always clean and neat, which was more than we were. After about eighteen months they moved away and we were allowed to move into their cottage in addition to our own. And now we were really grand.

We now had a fair-sized living room, a scullery with a stone sink and a cold-water tap, and two bedrooms, in addition to the original two small rooms. And the sole use of the privy down the garden. Our old rooms went practically out of use, and each winter we used the

24

upstairs room as a playroom. It is surprising what you can do in an entirely unfurnished room, if you are not too much overlooked. We carted rubbish from goodness knows where up those stairs, Dith had her side and I had mine, till she tired of it. I was always trying to make things — talk about bricks without straw — and would cut chairs and beds and dolls' prams out of cardboard boxes, cut furniture catalogues to pieces and paste the results onto card, making rooms, and cut ladies and children out of fashion books, and sets of clothing and dress them and have families and shops and schools.

The winter weekends were often very happy for then, if I were not in disgrace with someone or other for something or other, Doff would play with us as well. We played schools and wrote compositions and poetry. Doff was very good at this and so was I, and we loved it, but poor Dith was not quite so good, and between the two of us would get rather frustrated, and insist that I hadn't written that poem but remembered it from school. Mother used to go to bed after dinner on Sundays, and we made tea about five o'clock and took it up to her, and these happy afternoons sometimes ended in clouts or being sent off to bed. After a good rest Mother liked nothing better than a good row, in which Dith could nearly hold her own — except for Mother's heavy hand — and at any sign of a squabble would come down on us both like a fury, demanding to know was she never to have peace in her own home after all these years, shriek and tear her hair and finally drive us with telling slaps into outer darkness, after which Dith dealt with me. Dorothy, of course, was never included in these scenes, but stood with a frozen, pale face, looking on, and disapproved of me still more, for Mother was always a little heavier on Dith than on me.

CHAPTER
FOUR

I have a very clear picture of Mother in those days. She was fairly dark, with dark brown hair which I never saw her wash or brush, an excellent skin and bright colour, and brown, bright, snapping eyes which, until she was old, always sparkled. She had a scar across her lip which she blamed on Father. She never bathed, nor washed below her neckline, and she smelled. She was slightly above average height, and carried herself with a jaunty, swaying kind of swagger, with her head held very high. Her neck was badly scarred from an operation for tubercular glands, and she wore a black band to hide the scars above her stiff uniform collar — she wore striped dress or apron, with collar and cuffs for her work. Her relations with other people were not good; with her employers she was obsequious, with underlings, alternately bullying and familiar. She would pretend to be a widow, and then, when on familiar terms, tell all her past history and regret it afterwards. So everyone knew that she had left her husband, which just was not done in those days, and that we had been in institutions. She professed to despise the village people, which didn't help in making them any more friendly towards us, and when she did pay a man a few pence for doing a small job, like scything the grass, was very patronising and suspicious; but she had a natural hatred of men and despised women. She was intelligent but despotic and bitter, and had a harsh, instant temper that battered down anyone weaker than herself. I don't know if she ever wanted affection, but she could neither show nor receive it. She might have done to Dorothy whom she really loved, but then Dorothy could not make a fuss of anyone either, and certainly not of Mother, against whom she not unnaturally felt resentment, and whom she feared. I did need love and at first turned to Mother for it, but was always pushed away and told that she didn't want "cupboard love".

Her road of escape was reading; very soon there were heaps of books, probably from jumble sales, of all kinds, good novels and trash, all over the place. She, and the other two for that matter, would sit in the middle of any kind of muddle, with unwashed dishes, unmade beds, burning food, or none at all, and lose themselves in someone else's adventures. She vented on us, day in and out, her vitriolic hatred of our father, and in lesser degree, of all men, and I grew up with a deep rooted fear of them, at the best, and an inferiority complex towards them that was no help to me in later life. I think we were all affected by it. She carried on a constant guerrilla warfare with the man who kept the engine room at the laundry, who would not acknowledge her overlordship, and as he was the brother of quiet Mr Hatley next door, this extended, to some extent, to our relationship with them.

She never praised us, took no pride whatever in our appearance and had no standards for us at all, except for our morals. No children brought up in a convent could have had less knowledge of the world than we had. We knew no men or boys, and she tried to keep from us any books which mentioned sex, no easy matter. I can remember now certain books which I was forbidden to open on pain of terrible penalties, and had the most extraordinary ideas of what they were about. There was one called *The House with the Green Shutters*, with a lurid picture on the cover of a woman running away, with her clothes streaming from her, from something or other, and I was terrified even to see it lying about. Dith read them all, of course, quite soon, and appeared none the worse, but not me.

Quite soon after being at home we were thoroughly dirty, of course, and had "things in our hair", but I don't think our bodies became verminous again. We did have hoppers in our beds, but not lice. Possibly our cottage was free from them when we went in, and soon I really did keep it quite clean, but I am surprised at how long it took me to acquire any standard of personal cleanliness. I cannot remember how I was dressed when I left the Institution, whether fitted out in their clothes or in some that Mother provided, but her idea of dress was most simple. An unbleached calico loose shift next to the skin, ditto long drawers — just two straightish legs stitched together at the top back and front, any old dress as a petticoat in winter and a larger one on top. For a long time everything possible came from jumble sales, but for some unearthly reason

Mother didn't buy children's clothes. We had to wear women's dresses with the skirts tacked up to our boot tops and the sleeves rolled up. She never mended anything, and we wore our clothes till they literally fell off. Curiously she took our undergarments to the laundry each week for washing, but they were so often in rags I don't know what the other women thought. Once or twice I remember a child's dress being given to me, and it always had to be kept for Sundays, when I invariably outgrew it. I remember one white broderie anglaise dress, given to us with one sleeve very badly torn; all the bits were still there, but it was never mended. I loved it and wore it, rags and all, on Sundays until I could no longer squeeze into it. Normally we didn't wear hats, but I can remember one winter going round in a charming grey beaver bonnet, a poke one, and have an idea it was most old-fashioned; I certainly remember it as "Cranford-ish", and with my loopy long skirts and woman's coat and hob-nailed boots, must have looked a most extraordinary little object. We were great figures of fun to the other children for a long time, but fortunately we lived out of the village, and it was only the walk to school I dreaded. I would wait as long as I could hoping to miss the boys who baited us, but sometimes they would wait and run round us as we went along mocking and jeering. This always reduced me to tears, but Dith would give them as good as she got. They often threw stones at us, and once Dith got in first and scored a lucky hit. The boy ran off howling but he and his mates went to the headmaster and complained that we had said nasty things and thrown stones, so Mr King came across from his desk and boxed my ears, saying I sat there, looking like an angel, instead of which I was a little devil. He didn't say anything to Dith though. One day the boys caught me by myself and threw handfuls of burrs at me, and I arrived at school with my short curly hair standing out stiff with them. The junior teacher had to spend the morning getting them out, which she did, and quite a lot of my hair with them.

Then suddenly Mother started making clothes for Dith and me. She produced the first frocks, one each, during her week's holiday in the summer, and we were terribly excited. They were of cotton material with sprigs of flowers, mine was pink and Dith's lavender, and as she had no machines, sewed them by hand with very large, loose stitches. They were cut "out of her head" and had a top with sleeves all in one piece, and a full long skirt fastened on to the top with several rows of gathering stitches which she called gauging. This design had an awful weakness: we would tread on our bottom hems, which would part from the front of the yoke with a dreadful "rrrrip", and hang down even further, disclosing our frightful underneaths. The skirt would be anchored on to the top again with pins. The tapes of my drawers were generally missing too, and if anyone had come near me with a reasonably strong magnet, I think my clothes and I would have parted company. When the winter was coming Mother got busy again, and produced two more dresses, same design, of a fawn serge. These had long sleeves but the same inherent weakness so we were not over-decent for long. These, I think, were meant to be our Sunday dresses at first.

The only mending of any kind that I recall was of "footing" stockings. We never had new ones, and as our old ones were always in holes, re-footing was a constant evening chore. To re-foot, you cut the worn part of the foot from a woman's stocking, inevitably making it shorter, and leaving only the instep part of the foot. From another stocking you cut out a piece roughly the shape of the sole of the foot and stitch it on to the instep part of your stocking and then onto the leg. You now have a tube sewn up at one end, which you pull up your leg and hey presto, you have a new stocking, baggy for a child, with no ankle to speak of, and with lumps inside where the footpiece has been very roughly sewn on, causing horrible blisters under hobnailed boots, but your legs are covered as long as you have a piece of tape or string to tie round the stocking tops. We never rose to the dignity of garters.

I have not mentioned someone who loomed quite largely in the background of our lives at this time. To me she was never anything but a name, Miss Bardsley. She was a welfare worker in London, and must have been in touch with us first through Jessie's schoolmistress, who probably contacted her when Mother first left. She fixed Jessie up with somewhere to live and then at a Girls' Friendly Society hostel until she was earning enough to make her own plans, and was somehow concerned with tracing Mother, and encouraging her to get us together again. She was the source from which the "hamper" emanated, and from time to time there were red-letter days when a parcel came from Miss Bardsley. The material for these dresses came from her, and the first girls' shoes we ever had, which unfortunately did not stand up to our wear for very long.

Soon after the Stubbinses left, our second summer, I think, Jessie was unwell, and through Miss Bardsley's arranging, came down for two weeks holiday. It doesn't seem possible as I look back, but she disliked us all as much as ever, and did not speak to us if she could help it. We were at school, of course, in the daytime, and she lay in the garden reading, or sat in the apple trees and when we were home took herself off for walks, sometimes with Doff. Then after a meal she went to bed. I don't think Jessie and Mother had one conversation together, and there was a most uncomfortable atmosphere when they were both in the house; they were as implacable as ever towards each other. Jessie must have been about seventeen, and was a shorthand typist in a publishing firm. She was dark-haired, rather like Mother in looks, but much shorter. After she returned to town we had a wonderful parcel from her. A book each, the first new books we had ever owned. I had Ward Lock's *Wonder Book*, Edith had *Grimms' Fairy Tales* and Dorothy had *John Halifax, Gentleman*. For years I knew nearly everything in my book by heart. One full-page picture of a smiling, beautiful fairy lady, surrounded and studded with stars, and with the caption "The Evening Star, Guardian of the Night", was a comfort and delight to me. Lying in bed in the dark I would picture her lovely soft face, with silver stars spangling her hair, and think she was sitting up there in the dark sky, looking after me.

Religion, the belief in a God who loved me and gave himself for me and my sisters, did not come into life at Felsted. We had Bible-reading at school, and in fact read the Bible ourselves a good deal and found it fascinating though long winded — the Old Testament rather than the New — and we went in a desultory fashion to Sunday School. I am rather afraid it was when a treat was in the offing, but the reception we got was not calculated to make us want to go more unless we were going to get something out of it. My class was held in the church, on a dozen or so chairs in one corner. I don't remember the teacher, but I do remember the vicar on one occasion looking at me as if I were a particularly loathsome toad that had crept in surreptitiously among his nice clean lilies, and saying "Yes, you would come now, wouldn't you?" On telling this indignantly to Mother, we were not sent for a Sunday or two, but Dith and I were sent to the party; though allowed in by the lady at the door — presumably she didn't know us — we were spotted later by the vicar, scowled at and severely ostracised, and not allowed to have the bag of sweets and the orange with which all the others were presented at the end. I also remember a glorious treat in Pleshy. I think this was provided by one of the wealthy local farmers for all the village children. We met in his big sweet-smelling farmyard, which was on the station side of the village, and were loaded onto great high slatted-sided wagons, with wide sideboards. We were jammed together so we couldn't rattle about, but those of us who were lucky were lifted up onto the sideboards; I was one and in my glory. I don't remember if there was more than one wagon load but my memory shows me a procession of carts, each pulled by four massive carthorses, rolling at a stately pace through the narrow lanes with high hedges on either side which we could lean over and touch, with long breaks in between showing fields of golden stubble — from which I deduce it was an after-harvest celebration. The sun streamed down, and I had on my white frock with the torn sleeve and felt wonderful. There is a hazy impression of lots of races and running about and being organised, and then a great tea in a barn, long tables and lots of bread and butter and buns, and mugs of tea. Then replete with sunshine and food, back into the wagons and the slow, clopping journey home, with all the bigger ones singing and shouting their heads off, "We've all be . . . en to Pleshy, we've all be . . . en to Pleshy, we've all be . . . en to Pleshy, and had a lovely day." We certainly had, though I don't know how those of us who had quite a distance to walk, managed to stagger home from the farmyard where we were put down, but it was worth it.

One of our greatest joys at Felsted was the farm nearly opposite our cottage. The farmer, Mr Smith, didn't live there, but about a mile away at Bannister Green, where his wife had a thriving village shop. They had three boys who went to boarding school and only came home for the holidays, when they were often at the farm. They each had a pony, and used to ride up with their father and be around the farm buildings and fields with him. The house, a lovely period place, was occupied by a master from the public school and one of the grown Stubbins girls was their maid. It was into a kind of courtyard at the back that we had to go for our water. First of all, opposite our garden, was the orchard, full of trees with a stream running through it; this emptied into a wider and slower stream which curved round to the road, and continued along by the roadside, bordered by little willows until it stopped at the long lawn which came down from the front of the house. Perhaps it had been culverted there, I don't know, but a stream certainly appeared at the bottom of our garden on the other side of the road, and continued its pretty way, bordered with milkmaids and full of watercress. Where the little stream joined the wider one, a charming wooden bridge had been built leading from the orchard to the farmhouse garden, and on the other side of the bridge the wider stream travelled on to the farmyard, where it emptied into a very large pond, almost a lake, in fact. We were very annoyed when the weather was severe in winter and the ice on the pond would bear, for no sooner had we started having a really good time sliding, than masters and boys from the school would appear with their skates and we were driven away.

Still, we used to slide to our hearts' content on the strip of ice that led from the roadway, under the bridge through to the farmyard, and were never disturbed there. Once the ice broke and Annie Stubbins went through to well over her middle, but we hauled her out

— I think a brother must have been around to help — and as she came out we noticed a tiny piglet in the broken ice. I expect it was one that had died at birth, but it's not nice to have dead piglets stuck on one.

All the year round that water was a happy playing place. It wasn't deep and we made rafts, or rather pinched things lying around which would serve as rafts, and where it was narrow enough for us to keep hold of a willow branch, actually floated on the water and imagined adventures galore. Milkmaids grew there, and moorhens nested on the banks, and there were hundreds of birds and lovely fluffy water rats. We played in the farmyard mostly at weekends, I imagine, romping in the stockyard; and the cart shed by the farmyard gate was a particular haven. One could play anything, imagine anything, in those great high wagons. I know I had quite a job climbing up into them. Mr Smith was always pleasant to us when he saw us; and none of his men interfered with us; and when we kept chickens and one of our hens laid away in his haystacks, as the silly things were always doing, he would gather up the nest and the eggs and the clucking, grumbling hen into a box, and send them back. Once a hen had a clutch of sixteen on the point of hatching when she was found, and he waited till the chicks were out, all sixteen of them, and brought them himself with a pleasant word about them. Later he kept turkeys and they formed the habit of coming over each evening and roosting in our trees, and though we were scared stiff of the cock, who used to put feathers up and gobble dreadfully at us, Mother actually didn't grumble and let us go and report, and Mr Smith finally put them in a shed at night.

Our other paradise was the stretch we had from the bottom of our garden, which we entered through a hole we made in the hedge. It was generally soggy and muddy there, for the stream ran close, but we made for the gate at the end of the field and through another one to the wood. The first field, as I said, had the stream with milkmaids and kingcups, the second, at one side, a bank, thick and fragrant in spring with white violets. I have never seen the like anywhere else. Primroses started as one neared the wood, which itself was spread with a carpet of them patterned with mauve anemones.

The small stream reappeared round one side of the wood, and I spent long hours there, ankle-deep in mud, damming the stream and floating pieces of wood, and having races with them. It is curious to me how, feeling inferior as I know we did, we should yet have taken such complete possession of the farm and fields. They could not have given us more exquisite pleasure had they belonged to us. As a matter of fact, we did not understand possession, and in our minds they did belong to us, and when in the finest weather, an occasional group of schoolboys in their speckled straw hats came through on a Sunday afternoon walk, we were most indignant. We used to go out early and gather mushrooms too, little milk white buttons with pale pink ruching underneath. Mother and the others were very fond of them, but they used to give me tummy ache.

School was a place where, once I ceased to worry about the remarks from the other children about my personal appearance and sanitary drawbacks, I could lose myself and be completely happy — perhaps I should say "find myself", for I found learning a most easy and satisfying thing — and as I was, in spite of everything, really quite inoffensive, the teachers had nothing against me. We had three of them in the big school: a junior, Miss Francis, Miss Wallace who took standards three and four, and Mr King, the headmaster who didn't like girls and showed it often very plainly. After a settling-down period, I romped through the school, though I rather fancy the demands on us were not very great.

In those days one learned one's grammar, tables and history parrot fashion and I had an unusual memory. We sat with our arms folded, chanting "nine ones are nine" to "nine elevens are ninety-nine —" gulp "an' nine twelves are nundred neight" gulp "ten ones are ten" — and so-on through the gamut; sometimes the teacher would go out of the room for quite a while but we chanted on. My grammar comes to me naturally, though I don't know the science of it, and the history I learned at school was of the Alfred and the cakes variety. Geography was a matter of a yellow curling map of the world on the wall, and Miss Wallace pointing out names with her long pointer, while we chanted them after her, but why, I never really sorted out.

I did learn though that all the red places on the map belonged to England — not Great Britain — and had been won for England by our men who had gone out to strange places and fought and died to annex them for England. I was English, therefore they belonged to me — this business of possession again. I, a no-account waif, was as proud of my English blood as any highborn lady, and this pride remains with me still, reprehensible though it may seem to the present generation. (I have never managed to reconcile the Welsh part). But at an early age I could recite all the counties of the British Isles with their county towns. I did maps well but not because I understood them. It was only a matter of copying out of a book and I was good at drawing. I began to come out very big in the yearly examinations, and before I was eleven was put into the top class, where Dith was, to her intense disgust. For this feat, to my great astonishment, I was given a book as a prize at the annual prize giving. All parents were invited, of course, but only the nicest ones went, or those whose children could be expected to be among the elite. Dith and I sat in everyday clothes among the neat girls in their best dresses, and when my name was called out I was terrified. For a moment I wondered what crime I was to be punished for, and tumbled up to Mr King's desk, bitterly conscious of my sloppy stockings and loopy skirts. But he actually smiled at me and said "To Gertrude Roberts for unusual applications and merit". It was quite a fat book, with a decorated bookplate inside the front cover, with my name and PRIZE printed on it, and the date and the reason for the award. When I recovered from my fright I was exalted, but this soon evaporated. Before we reached home Dith had pretty well pricked the bubble of my self-esteem, and the indifference of the others demolished it entirely. Doff resented a slight to Dith and Mother said she had had enough of that sort of thing with Jessie. My precious book was lost to me, with other treasures, when we left Felsted, for Mother always had to travel light for financial reasons.

In the top class we worked alone a lot as Mr King was busy, working sums from cards, and writing compositions and, a pleasure to Dith and me but a bore for the others, silent reading. Just as I went into the class, a lot of new books had arrived, and these were issued one at a time for us to keep in our desks, to be read between set tasks. They were very good — most of Dickens, Scott and Charlotte Brontë, and others. How I loved *Ivanhoe* and *The Mill on the Floss* and *Pickwick Papers*, but much of Dickens was too intolerably real to me to be called enjoyable, though I read most of them. *Bleak House* and *Little Dorrit* were harrowing, but the one I could not read was *Oliver Twist:* that, and *The Old Curiosity Shop* I have never been able to read through. I saw myself in *Jane Eyre*, only more so, and wondered what she was fussing about. Before long Mr King told me there was nothing more he could teach me, and in the mornings I would be sent to his house to help his wife, who was the infant teacher. This was a way of getting cheap labour, of course, but it was the first nice home I had been into, and seemed wonderful to me.

Mrs King was kind and loved little girls as much as her husband disliked them. She had one son and would talk, as I peeled potatoes, about her little boy Frank, but I did not realise then that the large man in the chauffeur's uniform, who slipped in often for a cup of coffee, was him. He frankly terrified me, and when Mrs King became confidential and told me what a pity it was Frank's wife couldn't have children, I just didn't know what she was talking about; but she never realised that. I just had no idea of family relationships at all. She was a soft, plump dump of a woman with dimples, who took us for singing once a week, and always had me out in front to show the others how to do it: once we had a little school concert; I sang a solo, "A Country Life is Sweet" — of all things. Mrs King landed me in a big row once. There was no cottage nearer to the school than ours, and as they were going away for a fortnight's holiday she asked me to look after her cat, to give it milk night and morning, and she gave me a shilling to pay for it. I gave the money to Mr Smith, and each day trotted up to the schoolhouse with half a can of milk that I put in the cat's dish. It was holiday time, no-one bothered about what I was doing, and I made myself very much at home in the garden looking at the flowers and eating the fruit. But when Mrs King returned she brought me a present, a picture of Ventnor in a red plush frame stuck all over with shells

This started Armageddon. First, I had spent the money and fed the cat on our milk. Second, why had I been such a fool as to give the money to Mr Smith when I could have taken some of our pennorth of milk for the cat, and handed the shilling in to Mother. Third, I was a deceitful, sly cat not to tell anyone anything about it, and fourth, I was not allowed to have the picture, it belonged to the family. I was really in the doghouse for weeks and Edith would just not let it die. I didn't emerge until Mother found I was having constant nosebleeds, and it eventually came out that Dith was experimentally knocking me on the nose to make it bleed so she could slip a cold key down my back to make it stop. It so happened that after a few times the bleeding didn't stop, and I bled long enough to get them worried, and I had to be taken to the doctor. Mother was very fond of experimenting on both of us, rather liked to see us squirm, I think, and I could always be depended upon to give full value for money.

We didn't have baths in a zinc or wooden tub by the fire as the other children did; it would have been impossible to heat the water as we hadn't vessels big enough, but Mother got a craze once for us to have cold baths, Dith and me. She filled the wooden tub with cold water and we were supposed to jump in and be sloshed down. Dith, after a bit, would grit her teeth, jump in and straight out again, run away and give them no fun; but I, silly little wretch, would create and shiver and cry and eventually by the time Dith came back, be picked up and plonked in and held down, where I screamed and splashed and gave them all a really good laugh.

Another family joke was my weekly taking of pills. I had a funny tummy and Mother used to try out various patent medicines, usually pills. I have always found it difficult to swallow even a small hard substance at will, and when Mother put a Beecham's pill on my tongue and commanded me to swallow, I couldn't. There was no jam or drink to help it down, and Mother would try different things, such as holding my nose, or pressing the top of my head and under my chin to keep my jaws still, and they laughed till the tears ran when the sugar coating had gone and I began to retch with the bitter taste. Some other time Mother discovered sulphur and treacle — the same as Mr Squeers used — and a weekly dollop of that was much better than those dreadful pill sessions, and probably did us a lot of good.

We had a wonderful treasure trove up at Felsted School. In the yard, just inside one of the back gates — a servants' entrance — was a large refuse vehicle, I cannot describe it better. Each term when the boys were breaking up, they obviously had to clear out all their surplus books and belongings, which were put in here. Each day we would go through the gate to this vehicle, climb up on the step, lean over and help ourselves. Once we found this we never lacked for books. There were, of course, many we could not understand, the Greek, Latin and French grammars for instance, but there were oh so many boy's books of adventure, Henty, Kipling and Marriott, *Midshipman Easy*, *Masterman Ready*, *Robinson Crusoe* and *The Swiss Family Robinson*, dozens of them every term, and magazines galore; *The Strand* and *The Windsor* were my favourites because they each carried reproductions of pictures and lovely poems. One picture I have never forgotten was of a rocky coast in a gale, with seagulls wheeling in the wind and the poem underneath was

Listening now to the cry of the sea with its
   broad-flung shipwrecking road,
Now to the scream of a maddened beach, cut
   down by the wave.

It was by a famous artist and the poet was Tennyson, of course. I cut it out and stuck it on my half of the wall in our room. My biggest treasures were Scott's *Lay of the Last Minstrel*, and a slim green leather volume of Shakespeare's *King John* — I broke my heart over Prince Arthur. I managed to hang on to these books, they were so small, and have them still. *King John* has an inscription on the flyleaf "To dear David from his loving Aunt Elisabeth"; many of the books had similar messages in the front. I am glad the donors did not know what little store their nephews set by their gifts, but they certainly gave us much happiness. One day when I was standing on my head in this vehicle, just my rump sticking out, I received the full contents of a bucket of cold water which some humorous servant flung out of an upper window. I and the books I had salvaged were drenched, and I beat a hasty and dripping retreat.

We kept two half-holidays at school, May Day and Oak Apple Day. On May Day we assembled as usual, the register was called and then — it was a fine day, naturally — we filed out and went for a long walk through the fields behind the school. The hedges were fragrant and white with May blossom, and it would seem you couldn't put a pinpoint between the flowers in the grass and on the banks, and the air was full of birdsong. Mr King seemed to be a different man and talked to us about the flowers and birds, and showed us a lark's nest on the ground, and dared any boy to come back and rob it. The whole blessed morning was spent picking flowers and wandering about, and when we got back to school we were released for the rest of the day.

On Oak Apple Day — I have forgotten the date — the day King Charles hid in the oak tree and so eluded his pursuers, we went out into the fields, on the other side of the road from the school, to an open place where oak trees stood and each found an oak apple. Not until we each had one did we continue our walk, and so back to school. The boys had a grand time climbing the trees and finding oak apples for the girls, and I suspect were not nearly as quick as they might have been, but on this day Mr King did not mind. The morning was our half-holiday and we had lessons again in the afternoon; I never forgot about King Charles, and if you want to know, the tree he hid in is the very large one on the right, the first you see as you come out of the Long Meadow opposite the school.

Once a year at Felsted there was pea-picking. The school holidays were timed to fit in with this, and then the social distinctions were seen very clearly. "The poor" went pea-picking, the others didn't. We were wakened by an alarm clock before dawn, dressed ourselves more dead than alive in the dark, took our bread and jam which we had got ready the night before, and tumbled out to the field which was never very far away. There were plenty of other people, women and children, there already. We each took a sack from the man at the gate, took up the position in the line that he set us, and proceeded to pick; the correct method was to pull up a plant with the left hand, smartly pick off all the pods with the right and drop them in the sack, depositing the "rice" as the empty plant was called, smartly behind one. One walked forward, picking to right and left and in front, and some of the pickers were very deft and quick. Needless to say, we weren't and never kept up with the line, but some sensible woman would always pick some of ours to keep the line straight, though we always felt she should put the peas in our sack, not her own. We were paid one shilling for a well-filled sack; the man in charge knew all the tricks, and would pick up an apparently well-filled sack by the corners, bang its bottom on the ground once or twice, and hey presto, it was not three quarters full. Mother would bring us a jug of tea on her way to work if she could and we went home to dinner. It seems it was sunny all the time, and though we became very tired, I expect we rested quite a bit, and enjoyed it; though of course, we had to pick our quota or we should not have been allowed to come again the next day.

Miss Wallace, the schoolteacher, had a very sad life. She had been a pretty girl — and was still quite nice looking, but old in our eyes — and had been engaged to be married to a young master at the school, but her father, an apparently well-to-do business man, became involved in some scandal like misappropriating funds or something and committed suicide when found out. The young man broke off the engagement, Miss Wallace's mother became a permanent invalid, and she herself had to earn a living for them both by working as an uncertificated teacher in the place where everybody knew her story.

CHAPTER
FIVE

When the Stubbinses left, we had a piece more garden, and Mother bought a hen with a sitting of eggs, and put her in a box in a little shed we had. We hammered some light, wooden posts into the ground and put some wire netting round — pretty roughly, as it was always falling down — and we "went in" for chickens. We were surprisingly successful, chiefly due to the fact that when the hens wanted to sit, they just got out and laid away and then came back with their families. We used to walk to the mill at Bannister Green for barley meal and maize — we acquired a box on wheels to carry it. The mill was a wonderful place with great sails and everything covered with a grey-white coat of wheat dust, including the miller. He was a cheerful, kind man who always seemed to be in a little room right up the top near the sails, and used to come, grey-white including his eyelashes, down a spiral staircase to serve us.

Most of the eggs were sold through people at the laundry, but we always had one each for breakfast on Sundays. Unfortunately, they didn't suit me as my tummy seemed to tie itself into knots, and Doff says I used to turn green. But the worst chore was when birds were sold for eating. I had to catch one, put it in a basket — we hadn't one with a proper lid — and keep pushing the thing's head in, then take it to a man in the village who would wring its neck. Then bring it back again and pluck it. Of all the jobs for a small inefficient girl, chicken-plucking must have been the worst. I had feathers from head to foot, up my nose, down my neck, and for a long time it took me hours to do. Of course, I was not supposed to tear the bird's skin, and it was most difficult. On one occasion I thought I wouldn't bother to take the bird down to the village, but would wring its neck myself, as I had seen the man do, but I wasn't strong enough, or hadn't the knack. I held the bird as tightly as I could against myself with my left arm, grabbed the top of its neck just under the head with my right hand, and pushed my knee in the middle, but the bird didn't play fair. All it would do was screw its head round, roll its wicked little eye at me and say "qr-r-r-r". Then it got away and I had to catch it again and put it in a sack — easier than the basket — and go to the village after all. Finally we had more birds than we could cope with, and quite a few were sold to the Bursar at the school. This meant that Mother and Doff had to join in the plucking, which they did not like at all, and the numbers were allowed to die down again to one or two.

When the chickens were grown just past the fluffy stage, they were always trying to get through the wire, and often one would get caught by the leg which would be broken. We would bring it in — this was Dith's speciality — and splint its leg with a matchstick and keep it indoors until the end rotted off, which it usually did, but the stump healed up and there were generally one or two dot-and-carry birds around. We used to bring wild baby birds in too, which had met with some accident, but never managed to save one. They would have been better without out gentle ministrations, I think. We would push food down their wide baby beaks — generally bread and milk, as being the one invalid food we knew — wrap them up and put them in a cardboard box to keep warm. On one occasion Dith put one in the oven which wasn't very hot, but forgot about it and when the fire was made up, it cooked.

Dith left school the term before she was thirteen, and also went to work in the laundry, and now my life became very much happier. I was very happy alone, doing my jobs and running my errands without the irritant and fear of her in the background, and I am afraid I formed one or two very bad habits. I never had any money of my own except my Saturday ha'penny, and I discovered I could "fiddle" change a bit, and buy myself a ha'penny strip, or some bulls' eyes, and there was no Dith to see what I was doing. Also I found it easy in the baker's shop (which was also an excellent sweet shop much used by the school boys) to pick up an occasional chocolate bar or whipped cream walnut when no-one was looking, and slip it into my basket. I got away with it for a while, but one day to my horror, as I strolled home chewing something that could not be disposed of in a hurry, there was Dith coming towards me. She had had a bilious attack, and been sent home, but could not get in as I had the key. As I had eaten most of the purloined sweet, there was nothing in it for her, so she kept me on tenterhooks with threats for days, and then "told". The family had a really good time on that again, and Mother had spurious hysterics, demanding to know what she had done that her daughter should be a thief! Still, everything passes, which thought has been a great comfort to me from time to time.

Occasionally, Mother and Dorothy went to London for the weekend and stayed with Aunt Emily, and Dith and I stayed alone. The first time I remember their going, when we were small, we had half a pound of sausages for our Sunday dinner, but on the way back from the butcher's Dith ate hers raw. I copied and ate one and was sick so we dined that Sunday on one fried sausage between two. From time to time we walked into the nearest town, which was six miles away, six long, weary miles for very young legs. There was a street market, and Mother would shop, we would have a cup of tea and a bun at a stall, and laden with parcels trudge back. It was of course, far too long a walk for our young strength, and we would be nearly fainting with fatigue before we turned the corner by the school into the straight stretch to our cottage. It was always dark too, before we reached home.

Several happy or amusing things stand out from those years. One happy one was that Mother, when in a good mood at a winter weekend, would make toffee, and was very good at it. We would all stand round while she boiled up the sugar with a dash of vinegar, over the fire, stirring all the time like a witch over her cauldron, and the lovely smell of boiling sugar permeated the house — there were no extra refinements like butter or flavourings, plain sugar was enough for her. Then she would pour it out, bubbling, into a greased tin, and we waited anxiously for it to cool, prodding it from time to time with exploratory fingers, so that always had a sort of dimpled surface. When cold, a short tap or two on the underside of the tin, and out it would come, brittle, golden and succulent. Sometimes it went wrong and stuck, when it either had to be pulled out in long, sticky strands and eaten off the fingers, or one got a red hot tongue from licking the bottom of the tin to get one's share. She could also, if she felt like it, pull it out of the tin before it was properly cool, and hang it over a nail in the wall, and pull and spin it to lovely different textures and then cut it into small pieces. That was lovely.

Events took place in the village, which we were allowed to attend, the last year or so. One was the annual concert at Felsted School. There wasn't room for all the village as well as the boys, but there were seats at the sides for those who worked or whose parents worked at the school. The front and middle seats were occupied by masters and parents who had come for the day; the concert was the culminating point of Speech Day, I think; anyhow, there were very many grandly dressed ladies there. The boys filled the rest of the hall. The concert started with the least talented and most nervous, and worked up to the most experienced and poised. The boys in the audience were quite well behaved, but quite willing to help out any faltering artist; in the case of a lanky youth with a reedy tenor and wobbling Adam's Apple who sang "Dan Cupid Harth a Gaaardon" and kept forgetting his words, they helped him most generously — especially that bit at the end that goes up high: "God gra-hahnt that I" etc and he stood there with his face and neck bright red with effort, and his mouth wide open, and couldn't be heard above the din. There were several clever boys reciting in what was probably Greek and Latin, who gained decorous applause, one or two humorists most rapturously received, and a string quartet, the first string music I had ever heard; it was wonderful to me — I do not know if it was good or mediocre. Then we had a scene or two from Shakespeare with boys dressed as women, of course, and I accepted them as such, though it was rather disconcerting when their voices jumped from high to low. Perhaps the hall was badly ventilated, but from time to time the boys would chant together, the volume growing until you felt you could cut it with a knife, "window, window", until some flurried person would get up and, with a baleful look in their direction, open a window.

One of my bad adventures happened on the way home. Our way was through the playing fields and over a stile or two to the road, and home, not more than a quarter of an hour's walk. A knot of village boys was hanging about looking for mischief, and saw us come out and followed, teasing and jeering. Dorothy was then around fourteen, very pretty and quite interesting to them, but was too proud and too scared to speak to them. Edith cheeked them and I tagged along, and we quickened our steps as we neared the last stile which spelled safety. My two big sisters had outdistanced me and gained the road before I reached the stile, but as I mounted the step the foremost boy made a grab at me, caught my skirt and pulled. My skirts held, but the pin in my drawers didn't, and down they fell, round my feet. Seething with rage and mortification I stood there on the step, grabbed my dreadful garments and slashed those horrible youths round the head with them, while they rolled about helpless with laughter. Dorothy would cheerfully have left me there but came then and pulled me off the stile, while I gibbered with helpless rage and tears the rest of the short way home. She thought I was loathsome.

Another occasional entertainment was the Penny Readings, held at the village hall. In exchange for our penny, we were presented with a programme of chaste items by local performers, introduced always by the vicar. These were by way of being a real night out for the local youths who would assemble at the back, and get a real pennyworth of fun out of putting the performers off by catcalls, so-called encouraging remarks, and downright barracking. The singers were always so very "refaned" and sang as though they had plums in their mouths. I remember a very large lady in evening dress liberally hung about with jewellery, who advanced to the front of the platform, arranged her immense bosom, settled her chins, and with her words held most obviously in front of her sang in a tiny little voice about "Three green bonnets at church one day, Dulcie and Daisy and Dorothy May". The remarks from the back about those poor girls were enough to put anyone off and she retired, red as a beetroot in high dudgeon.

While the noise was still at its height she was followed by a man who was introduced as a well-known professional; he was apparently visiting in the neighbourhood. He just stood there looking pleasant until the noise died down then held up his hand, said "Good evening" and began to sing "Old Simon The Cellarer". You could have heard a pin drop; every word was clear, no fancy vowels here, and when he had finished they roared and stamped and called for more. As an encore he sang quite simply and quietly "Land of My Fathers" — needless to say he was a Welshman. Before he went off he just said, "Give them a fair hearing, chaps." There were some readings too. The Vicar's sounded just like his sermons, but someone else read from *Mrs Caudle's Curtain Lectures*! I had not the slightest idea what he was saying, nor what a curtain lecture was, but he waggled his eyebrows so, and his voice went right up and then right down, I thought this very funny.

CHAPTER
SIX

The church, right down in the village, was old and beautiful with cottages clustering round it. They looked lovely but were very small for the overflowing families who occupied them. The School Houses where the boys lived, Senior House, Selwyn's, Morvan's and Junior, stood back from the village street, each a mist of rosy red brick, with their lawns and trees around them. Several charming Georgian buildings housed the masters, and there were quite a few neat cottages with gay front gardens, occupied by the more respectable working folk. The one pub I remember, the Fleur de Lys, stood back from the street behind a well-kept green, but somewhere near there were some pretty dreadful rows of one-up one-down cottages, all of them full to bursting with children large and small, some clean and some dirty, according to the woman in charge. I noticed very young that a man could be lazy or hardworking, drunk or sober, but the condition of the home and children depended basically on the mother.

I remember hot, sweet-smelling summers that seemed to go on for ever; bitter winter days when one woke in a completely unheated house to windows thick with ice inside, and bedroom slops frozen in the pail — we didn't possess chamber pots. Our tap would always freeze, and the sink waste too, and the journey over to the farm pump would start again. It was fun sliding on the road puddles as one went, but the frozen ruts were a hazard as one returned with the precious water. Harvest was a lovely time. The reaper and binder was the latest thing in agricultural progress, and we loved watching the great horses pull it round the field, the swathes of wheat falling gracefully as it passed, to be deftly handed out from behind, all ready in sheaves, which were stooked by the men following. Neither men nor horses ever hurried, all seemed to be done with a purposeful ease which was most satisfying to watch. And when they had finished, women and children came in to glean the fallen heads. We never had to do it, I don't know why not. Perhaps you had to have permission. There was no haymaking at Felsted; it was not cattle country, but most wonderfully productive for seeds. At the glorious Harvest Festivals I used to listen to the parable of the sower, and think farmers were among the elite who reaped not fifty, not sixty but a hundred fold.

I don't think I have ever seen since such Harvest Festivals. The church was not very big — though to me then it seemed immense — but every nook and corner and cranny was filled with the produce of the earth, not flowers, which the churches use to fill the gaps nowadays, but every vegetable and kind of grain possible; it was a job to get into the box pews without dislodging something. At the front of the nave was a mammoth loaf, flanked on each side with a great sheaf of wheat and at the top end of the aisle were two more immense sheaves. Barley, oats and Indian corn were there, too, all much taller than me. I could never make out, though, why there were no poppies, for surely they all went together. And the way people sang the Harvest hymns, full of deep thankfulness, I felt, and we joined in and rejoiced with the loudest of them.

Our Christmases, though pitiful by modern standards, were most happy. After all, who can measure happiness, even for children? It isn't a matter of how many gifts you shower on them. Our happiness was in the saving up of ha'pennies and pennies and planning and talking about what we would give each other; in gluing our noses to the little shop window where gifts were displayed, and wondering what our pennies would buy. Straw boxes, which on being opened displayed smaller ones inside, which in turn held smaller ones still, all in the gayest colours. Picture handkerchiefs, smelling richly of "dress" at two for a penny; sugar sweets in wonderful shapes and colours, harps and angels and animals; lovely cards of Mary and Baby Jesus and the manger, all picked out in gilt. The one I still have is not a folder card, but like a postcard and to me seems lovely. It was from Mother, and Doff gave me a little sixpenny Testament which I still have.

We hung our stockings up on Christmas Eve and Mother filled them — no talk about Father Christmas. She would put one of our russet apples in the toe, then some paper, then an orange — they were the very little, sour Spanish kind then, and my teeth still go on edge at the memory — then, with that funny streak of sadistic humour she had, a cinder or a large stone wrapped in the prettiest paper she could find; then a screw of boiled sweets, and in the mouth of the stocking each year we were at Felsted, a doll. How I loved those dolls! They had pink cotton bodies stuffed with sawdust and china heads and shoulders which were stuck over the bodies with glue. Mine always had fair hair and blue eyes; they were about ten inches high. The ends of their legs were black to resemble stockings, and they had little shiny shoes with buckles. Their arms had stitching at the end to look like fingers. They cost sixpence each, and unless one was very unfortunate and dropped them and broke the head, gave endless happiness. We girls gave each other our presents in bed too, before we dressed, and were always thrilled with what we had.

There was cooked meat of some sort for Christmas dinner, and a pudding, but we never knew Christmas cake or mince pies or any of the other things which I have since associated with the festival, but what we had was wonderful to us. Once we had one of our own "stumpy" chickens. Mother made us toffee apples after tea and while they cooled we would play all sorts of guessing games and there were most Christmassy things in the Christmas number of *Pearson's Weekly*, and a page which you had to heat at the fire, and if you were lucky a picture of something or other appeared, and you got a prize. We toasted ourselves pink over this, but nothing ever appeared. And there were competitions in the paper too, and limericks, and we all tried to do them. Then the highlight was roasting chestnuts on

60

the shovel, and eating some of our own walnuts; and when I did go to bed, cuddling my precious doll, I was so full up with the unusual treats and happiness that I wonder I slept at all. Christmas Day was a good day. On Boxing Day Mother did not go to work and stayed in bed most of the morning; but in the afternoon we had to watch our step, as her good humours never lasted long, and she would be more vindictive than usual to make up.

Once when Mother went to London to Aunt Emily's just after Dith started working, she brought a small second cousin of ours back with her for a holiday. She was about nine, but very small and colourless, with whitish thin hair and a pale sharp face, but we got on quite well together. Her name was Aggie, and the others ignored her. Her clothes seemed lovely to me, nice little check dresses and petticoats with lace on, quite a few of them, and soon in rags. She tried to help me with the house and liked the garden. Doff and Dith were sharing a room and bed now, and I was sleeping with Mother, which I hated. She would say, when she was undressing "Keep your eyes shut and don't watch me" — as if I wanted to — but I think she had to wear some sort of medical appliance, only of course I didn't know. Poor Mother. Anyhow, the old straw mattress came into use again. Aggie and I had it together in our old bedroom, and I liked her company well. She had a curious predilection for beds though. She would say she would go up and make our bed, and when some time afterwards I went up to see what had become of her, she would be lying on the bed with her knickers down and say "Come and do what the boys do". I hadn't the least idea what the boys did but she would show me to smooth the bottom of her tummy and her thighs with my hand. I found no pleasure in this, though I had no idea it wasn't seemly; I was willing to oblige but it seemed so silly, and after a time or two, left her to herself.

One evening I was getting supper ready and Aggie was upstairs as usual when I suddenly heard her scream, and she came tearing downstairs with the arm and shoulder of her dress blazing, and rushed to the door which was open. I can't say I thought of her, my reaction was that I would get into trouble. I tore after her, pushed her on the ground and rolled on her, beating the flames with my hands. Then I pulled the poor little soul into the kitchen, held her over the sink and poured cold water over her arm — well, pretty well all over her, so the smouldering didn't burst into flame again. She was grey and fainting and so cold I wrapped her in a big old coat and sat and cuddled her on a chair till Mother came in — not a very long time. All I could say was "I didn't do it. It wasn't my fault", but for once I was not grumbled at.

Someone went for the doctor who tut-tutted a lot over poor little Aggie's arm — I shall never forget the look of the charred flesh and dark pieces of burnt material stuck on it — and did what had to be done and dressed it, and told Mother to put her to bed and keep her warm. Then he looked at me and said "What about your hands?" and I was a heroine for five minutes while he bound them up and said "It's a good job she kept her head or you'd have a bit more to worry about." After that I had to take Aggie to the village every day to the nurse's house to have her arm attended to, and was away from school for several weeks. Mother didn't write and tell Aggie's mother what had happened, and it was about a month after the accident that she took Aggie home. It must have been a shock for her, but Aggie stoutly maintained that I had saved her life. So as far as I know, no-one was blamed. Her arm was dreadfully scarred and her neat clothes were all in rags, for they had disintegrated just as mine always did and no-one had mended them. I never saw Aggie again though we wrote a childish letter or two at first. They said Aggie had been playing with matches, but I could have told them. She had lighted herself with a candle on the floor while she "did what the boys did" and brushed her sleeve across it.

In our last year or two at Felsted we "acquired" a bicycle between us. Doff and Dith soon learned to ride, but I was not so quick. I had more of a job to reach the pedals, and besides, they did so love to see me fall off when they let go of the seat. But when Dith left, I had the bike to myself, except at weekends, and soon rode, and careered around on my errands very happily. My social status began to rise too. I found then and later that by myself I got on well with the village women. They accepted me, and would tell me how to do things, and I began to keep myself cleaner and neater. Then when pea-picking time came round and I didn't have to go to the fields, but could ride my bicycle past and see them and be seen by them, then my stock did rise.

About this time I developed my "family", an imaginative exercise which helped me and harmed no-one. I started, as they say "living in my imagination", and lived there on and off until I was seventeen. My name was Grace, not Gertrude, I had a loving father and mother, a younger sister and a pony. We lived in a charming house, every furnishing of which was real to me. We didn't have adventures, I just lived with, and talked to, this family whenever I could get away from the real one. I talked to them out loud out of doors, and remember once giving a farm man quite a shock. I was having a really animated conversation — we were out driving in the trap — when apparently hearing voices, he popped out from behind a haystack to see who it was and found only me. His face was a study! I used to go to bed as early as possible to be alone and lose myself, but typically no-one seemed to mind — or notice. As long as jobs were done, and they were free to read, they didn't take in much else.

On looking back at Felsted in those days, it appears to have been a mixed but prosperous sort of place. There were no landed gentry as I was to know later, but about three comfortable farms where the farmer himself worked and employed a number of men: and of course the school gave employment to quite a few, one way and another. The masters and their wives and families brought plenty of trade to the grocer and draper, butcher and baker, who were all private and old establishments. The butcher's shop was large and white, standing back from the road, with an open front, and carcasses hanging down on hooks which I could not bear to look at. At the side was a wide way leading to the slaughterhouse, and it was dreadful to pass when they were driving animals in. I had read that animals could always smell blood, and when they reared and bucked and tried not to go the way they were driven, I thought they knew what they were being driven in for. But somehow I never associated the meat on my plate with those woolly struggling things.

I realised later that the village people were not particularly moral, and also that several fathers preferred to bed with their young daughters than their worn-out wives, and there were some very mixed-up families at the village school. There were two village idiots too, one looked quite old and was merely a cheerful, gaping simpleton with tiny little eyes and a gingery mat of beard, but the other was rather horrid, a younger man with a face you couldn't bear to look at, who mouthed and gibbered and slobbered and shook. Most people were unkind to them and boys threw stones. There was a lot of cruelty to animals. Dogs dragged along tied behind carts, and on the hottest day having to run to keep up; and their ribs always seeming to stick out. In the yards dogs were always tied up; they didn't have any freedom, there was none of this "taking the dog for a walk" as part of the daily routine, and it was nothing to see a man or boy thrashing a dog with a stick. And as for the horses, I used to get into a terrible turmoil over them. The farm people were all right, of course; it was the small, odd traders who went round with their old, flat carts pulled by thin, knock-kneed, starved-looking horses, and carried great long lashing whips. The horses' skin would lie open in great weals, thick with flies, and the beastly men would sit there and lash at them and shout imprecations. I used to wish I could put them between the shafts and make them pull.

There was one horrible fat man who was a sort of odd job dealer in Bannister Green, who was the only man I remember seeing drunk there. He rode past our gate very frequently on a ricketty flat cart loaded with bits of old iron, pulled by a tiny, cowed, scraggy donkey, its ribs staring through its matted coat, and scars visible all over it. He would roll on the front of the cart and shout, and belabour the poor animal round the head with a great stick, while it put its ears down and kept its poor head as low as it could and tottered on. One night, for some unearthly reason, he came rolling up our path and in our door, and started being amorous to Mother. To our amazement, instead of pushing him out again, she looked coy, tossed her head and started being all feminine — our Mother! We were disgusted as well as scared, after all we had heard about drunkenness, and we combined for once and battered and shoved him outside, where we had great pleasure in hearing him fall over the chopping block.

One day when I was in Mrs King's kitchen shredding beans — they were new to me, we didn't raise such things at home — Mr King came in looking very serious and said I had better go home as my mother was not well. News spreads very quickly in country places, and as I went through the playground during morning break, it was obvious that most of them had heard some news. I was told by one that my Mother had had a bad accident; by another, more ghoulish minded, that she was all over blood and probably dead. I ran home as quickly as I could and found it was pretty bad, but not as awful as that. She had caught her hand in the rollers of a power-driven machine, and of course it had to stay there until the power was turned off. It was badly crushed and the palm nearly torn out, and I saw later she had a ring of stitches all round the palm. There seemed to be quite a crowd when I reached home. I don't know if she had been to hospital, but she seemed to be swathed in bandages, and was in bed. The nurse was there, and two of the ladies from the village, come to see if they could do anything. They soon felt unwelcome, I think, and went away and did not come back.

I don't remember how long Mother was away from work, quite a while I imagine, and the School people were good to her for those days, and paid her wages, but they found they could get along without her. She had an extremely neat, capable forewoman whom she detested, and she was quite able to manage with Dorothy, Dith and one old woman. When Mother did go back to work, she made the mistake of trying to get the school authorities to pay her a sum of money in compensation. I doubt if she took legal advice, but it was certainly a very foolish thing to do, for they just gave her a week's notice to leave, and her daughters too, so she was out of work. The Bursar was a good man who had always been kind and reasonable to her, and she tried him too far. In those days, when a woman had a job that suited her she hung on to it and took what came. That job had suited her and kept us together. However, with no money she now had to look for something else.

She got a job for Dorothy, pretty, ladylike Doff, as a laundry maid at some big institution at Redhill; Dith, that lanky hoyden just fourteen, went as a housemaid to a rectory in Devonshire — she who had not done a hand's turn in the house in her life. Some kind of an outfit had to be found for each of them, and when they had both gone we were without money. For a month we lived on credit, charity really, from the shops. I would creep round to them all in turn, for our pitiful bits, saying, "Mother would pay tomorrow", or next week or something. I cannot remember that I was ever refused, but oh, how my new-found pride suffered. Mother scanned the papers for jobs but it was an effort to find the pennies for the stamps. However, marvellously, a lady engaged her on the strength of the reference she had from the Bursar, or rather engaged the two of us, mother and daughter, to run the laundry at her big country house in Yorkshire. Fortunately she sent us the fare, or we wouldn't have been able to go. So on a cold day in December Mother and I went down to the village for the last time and went solemnly round to all the shops saying we were going away, but would send them the money we owed them. Of course we never did.

I fancy someone must have given us about five shillings for our small bits and pieces, for we broke our journey in London and stayed at Aunt Emily's for one night, and there was a bus fare to pay. I remember feeling terrible on the bus, and just as I was going to be sick, someone said, "Oh look at that girl, she's green". and I clenched my teeth and choked the vomit down again. I just would not call attention to myself any more. Consequently I went to bed as soon as we arrived and have never had the slightest recollection of Aunt Emily, her house or her family

CHAPTER
SEVEN

We arrived at Otley in the middle of a bitter afternoon in early December. I have no recollection of the journey. We stood looking out of the station entrance into a totally strange world. Somehow we were unprepared for the snow that had fallen, only a light covering, but enough to give a fairyland effect. The light came from below, not above where the sky was a heavy, dull grey. It was an effect I have seen since in the theatre where white lights at stage level send their beams upwards and outwards to pick up beauties or terrors in mountainous backcloths and sets. For me it was intensely beautiful and raised my spirits.

Felsted, in its soft, green, cultivated beauty had satisfied and comforted me, but the Chevin, rising up stark behind the station, its man-made ugliness smoothed over with the snow, going up and up until it was lost in the dull grey sky, was wonderful to me with a different kind of beauty. Here and there lights were beginning to prick out, and on a hidden road a single, slow moving spark showed where a horse and cart made a laborious way upwards. My heart began to sing, but not my poor mother's. She really hated the country anyhow, but this was terrible. She had been told we would be met, and I had visions of a carriage with a liveried coachman who would spring down and open the doors for us, but all we could see was a shabby cab of sorts, with a poor enough horse in its shafts. Fortunately no-one else needed it and the driver, in need of a fare, approached us. We had no money, but when he heard we were for Weston Hall, he was quite content to take us; so we and our hamper and paper parcels were loaded on board. There is little enough to record about this journey though it is etched on my memory in its strange whiteness. The greyness deepened as we progressed, and the light from the snow — which was thicker than had appeared at the station — was more unearthly. Instead of the soft hedges I knew, the roadside and fields were bounded by rough stone walls, and while we rode in a white carpeted valley, wherever I looked there were great hills, sloping away to infinity.

Once through the little town and over the river, the road was not much more than a lane, and we passed no house or cottage until we reached the great iron gates of Weston Hall. These were closed, but repeated shoutings from our driver produced a middle-aged woman from the Lodge hard by who, with many grumbles that she couldn't be expected to be on duty when the family was away, produced a huge key and let us in. It was about two and a half miles to the Hall from the town, but half this distance was through the great park, a rolling, hilly paradise, too extensive for me ever to explore wholly, going gently down to form a wide bed for the river on one hand, and rising in steep precipitous curves on the other, where it was bounded from the road by a high stone wall, which must have been miles in length altogether.

We cut through an avenue of great trees to the cavernous darkness of the servants' entrance. We found that the family was away, that instructions had been given for us to be met but no train time was given, that we were to go to the home farm where we were expected. Our driver was paid, the poor old horse urged out of the back gate of the estate up to a steep lane, bounded so closely with thick woods as to be a tunnel, to the tiny hamlet of Weston and the home farm. Here was comfort, a warm fire and a good tea, and we were welcomed, with reserve, by Mrs Saville, and me with enthusiasm by her daughter Evaline, who was a few months younger than me. I felt from the first she liked me and this outcoming on her part warmed me as much as the tea and fire. We were allowed to be friendly in a limited way, but it was not for two years that her parents trusted and began to care for me, and welcomed me in and gave me an insight into family life that showed me how things could be where love ruled and hate and bitterness were unknown.

It occurs to me here to say how different I found all the Yorkshire people from what I have ever since read that they are. To their own, intensely loving; to strangers they were suspicious, inhospitable and blatantly unkind. No beggar ever received a helping hand at those cottage doors, and woe betide any travelling salesman who tried his blarney on them. To the peddler they were a little different, for having no shops, they needed the tapes and cottons and needles he offered, but they stuck to the same man. No stranger need try to cut in on his ground.

A person from any other county, nay, any other Riding, was a "foreigner", and this in the proper sense of the word. They used it, and not as a joke. London people in particular were singled out. The men thought they were great humourists; all their so-called funny stories had the discomfiture of Londoners at the hand of "Yowkshire fowk" as their focal point: how some "champion lad" went to the great city and beat them all at their own game; or some "London Jim" came up to "Bratfort" with his pockets lined and went back with them empty; and they roared at their own humour. The women were on the whole hard-working and child-ridden, and had nagging, flaying tongues, which they used to great effect on their husbands when these worthies were hanging round the pump, gossiping on a sunny evening: but they never themselves came out to talk. Their lives were bound in four walls.

Their children were their joy and their desperation and riddled with TB. They were poverty stricken — the labourers were paid ten shillings a week with a cottage free. They had no gardens to grow vegetables, which had to be bought from the greengrocer who called each week. Their houses were tiny and airless with no sanitary conveniences save the outside privies, and no water except from the pump. I never saw a baby brought out of a house; they emerged from the dark well behind the open door on a warm sunny day when they could toddle, and sat on the doorstep. But if they could walk they were tethered in some way so they could not stray. Girls, when tiny, were pets, but soon turned into maids of all work out of school hours, but boys were adored and spoiled always. They tried to make me a butt for their witticisms and succeeded at first, for I was very trusting; I was well hoaxed by pigeons' milk which was very good for you if you got up early enough to get some. For many years I believed that the small black and white guinea fowl were peahens, and that "they didn't need no peacocks. They could do without". They called me London Jim, and never anything else until I was fourteen and their wives chid them. As in Felsted, the women ignored me for a long time, but then became kindly, giving me pleasant looks, and advice when I asked for it. "Eh lass, thou doos thee best," Mrs Train would say, "Thee'll learn," and I did learn, how to make bread and tea cakes — I don't remember flying any higher. I seem to remember that of the six families with children in that cluster of eleven cottages, seven children had TB and four of those died in the three years I knew them.

I found it difficult at first to understand their very broad speech, and as for them, the men roared at mine and mimicked me on all occasions. I was supposed to talk "la-di-dah" — at Felsted Dorothy had nagged me unmercifully if I slipped into the local idiom — and for a while I tried to cultivate a Yorkshire accent. I was succeeding quite well when Doff came back and stopped it with her contempt. It may sound curious to bring the village men into my recollections, but it was only the men who were hanging about in the evenings and Sundays round the pump with nothing to do, and who goaded and mocked a strange girl who was uncared for, who was twice as tall as their undersized progeny and who was naïve and completely ignorant of the things they and their children had always taken for granted. Their girls of twelve were adult in their knowledge of sex and babies. I knew nothing, but they wouldn't have believed that, and I have realised since that much of the conversation and many of the remarks tossed across at me would have caused Mrs Train's tongue to become a whip of scorpions had she heard them. Fortunately, as I didn't understand them, no harm was done. Train was always urging a couple of small boys of my own age to wrestle with me, and "throw me down", and not knowing the implications I once accepted the challenge, and threw the little wretch down myself; but I noticed the men's faces as I went into the fray, and saw the looks of sly, malicious contempt, and somehow was warned and drew away from them and, God help me, groped around in my mind for some reason for their attitude.

After tea we were given the key of our cottage, and although it was bright moonlight Mrs Saville lit us over with a lantern with a yellow tallow dip in it. These, I found later, one bought in bundles tied together by the wicks, not like white, separate candles I had been used to. A shock was in store, for of course we had no furniture, and for that one night we were loaned a mattress and two pillows. I realised afterwards how much out of character that lending was, and how feckless Mrs Saville must have thought we southerners were. I expect we produced bed linen out of the hamper and went to bed straight away, and in the morning went down the tunnel through the wood to our laundry, which was opposite the big back door of the kitchens, where Mother scrounged some breakfast for us. Mother was able that day to go and buy a bed and a couple of chairs, which was all our furniture for most of the time.

I don't know when the "Family" returned, but anyhow, we had a week or two to become accustomed to the laundry and the servants without too much hard work. There were eight women servants to wash for, in addition to the ladies' maid, who was away with the ladies, a butler, footman, valet and odd job boy. Mercifully we were supplied with striped uniform dresses and plain aprons, as were all the women servants — a neat pink stripe that made me feel very grand. I always loved pink. There were piles of sheets and tablecloths and teacloths and kitchen cloths, but what I hated most were the dozens of bloody cloths tied in bundles which Mother half-heartedly made a show of keeping away from me at first, but then didn't bother to, and when I moaned and asked what they were, said not to ask questions but get on with my work, I would know soon enough.

That first week we had leisure to go to Otley and lay in some food and a table. Later a couple of orange boxes were added. Whether these things were bought on "tick" or whether the butler gave us wages in advance, I do not know.

Even in the brightest weather the back entrance to the Hall was very forbidding, as it was shut in by woods that could not have been thinned for decades. On one hand a thick plantation of firs shut away the big open stretch of kitchen gardens, and on the other, glossy dark laurels, much higher than me, hid the spreading lawns which stretched up to the wide drive. This, coming round from the front of the house, led to the great wide steps up to the back door which the family always used when going out riding. The horses were led from the stables to the foot of these steps, and a beautiful picture they made with their gleaming necks and the satin of their coats. The groom stood holding their bridles, handsome in his navy and cream livery, and the family and their friends, so sure of themselves, so immaculate in their beautifully cut habits, their incisive high-bred voices floating up to the window from which I peered, well out of sight, alternately glorying in the picture they made and envying them bitterly for all that they were.

I should have said that a high wall ran along the edge of the plantation, right up to the corner of the Hall, and in the wall near this corner was the heavy wooden gate leading in to the big paved courtyard. I hated going through this door in the dark, for two big open wire cages were always placed on the ground, one on either side, to catch rats, and one could hear the squealing and squirming of the animals, and see the pinpoints of light from their eyes darting backwards and forwards and up and down, dozens of them jammed in together fighting to get out. I knew the head keeper later, and he was a kindly enough man, but to what he called "vermin" he was horrible. The rats would be released every morning in front of his dogs, and he and others stood around to stamp on any rat that looked as if it might get away. There was a gate and a clearing in the woody tunnel of the lane, and this was made dreadful with strings of little wild creatures, stretched on sticks, squirrels and weasels and stoats and rooks and jays and many others. If an animal wasn't something he was paid to preserve, then he considered he was paid to kill it.

On one side of the courtyard were the kitchens and servants' quarters, and on the other the laundry and the powerhouse. A full-time engineer was employed and the whole set-up must have been new and efficient, for there was never a breakdown in our time. Our machines all ran by electricity, and of course the lighting also. I had been in the big laundry at Felsted, but it was like a small factory compared to this miniature. Two things appealed to me: it was warm and it was clean. Most of the machines were plain wood, white with constant scrubbing which was done every day. The floor was tiled and also scrubbed daily, on one's knees — no pandering to laziness with mops — and the walls were washed every week. I don't know if the machines were modern for their time or not but there was still a great deal of hard physical work connected with the process of keeping clean the clothes for that community. The washing machines — there were two of them — were cylindrical, and consisted of an inner drum embossed with blunt wooden studs, and

78

an outer cover. The drum was filled with hot water and shredded soap — how I loathed shredding soap — each garment was soaped and put in, then the outer cover closed. A lever was pressed and the drum revolved, so many turns one way, so many the other, until it was turned off. During the process, if white cotton articles were being washed, the water was boiled for a certain time. Tragedy would have occurred if a small woollen or coloured article had hidden among the white ones; I can't remember it ever happening, but it was a possibility held in front of me with dire threats.

By one wall were four great wooden sloping-sided tubs on legs. These were for washing the ladies' finer garments by hand, for the woollens, for rinsing, blueing and starching — practically every cotton piece had to be starched, either boiled or raw, and the boiled starched things dried, damped and rolled. After the first washing was finished, each piece was run through large wooden rollers at the end of the machine, the water emptied and the process repeated two or three times. Then everything white went into the blueing tub, and then those that had to be starched were dealt with. There was a machine called a callender for pressing large things like sheets and bedspreads that did not require careful hand-ironing. This was like a large, very heavy table with a rail all round several inches from its padded top. At one end a thing like a giant rolling pin was threaded on this rail. One folded a sheet in two lengthways, laid it on the bed without a crease and curled one end round the roller and, pressing a switch for the heat, pulled a lever and the heavy roller travelled the length of the bed, winding the sheet round itself as it went; it then reversed itself and unwound, leaving a neat creaseless sheet which only had to be folded and hand-finished. With two skilled people working, this would happen every time, but when one was a clumsy girl of twelve, a good many creases and a good many tears were often the result. I was a tall girl for my age, but not the right height for the washing tubs, and I was soaked from my chest to my thighs every washing day, not to mention my arms where the water ran up them.

There was a strict order in which the washing was brought into the laundry. First the kitchen maid with all the stuff from the kitchen and the scullery maid with the rough aprons and oven-cloths; then the between maid with all the servants' clothing, the housemaids with sheets and bedding and towels and bits and pieces appertaining to any of the rooms, and the parlour-maid brought the table linen. The ladies' maid always brought the ladies' things herself, and a very pleasant person she was, and she often brought Col. Dawson's as well. He had a valet cum batman who had been with him in the army, and he and the maid had a great many privileges denied to the others. Our programme, to which we adhered strictly, was — Monday morning, receive and sort the gentry's clothes, whites, woollens, coloured, hand or machine; then the same with the servants' and the household stuff, but everything had to be kept religiously in its right category — you did not wash Mrs Dawson's camisole in the same water as the kitchen maid's!

Monday, Tuesday and Wednesday generally saw most things washed, dried and folded. We had to carry everything down to a small field which was our drying ground, about five minutes' walk away, a large wicker basket carried between us, and each with a smaller one tucked under the spare arm; it was a fatiguing business and many journeys had to be made, though I loved getting out into the air in the lovely breezy field. We sometimes met Col. Dawson as we walked and he would leer at Mother and she would simper and bridle at him and when we had passed, say "Old goat".

The rest of the week saw the things ironed and aired. The ironing room was very pleasant in that it was lofty and light, with three big windows. Two overlooked the courtyard — not so pleasant — and one, as I have said, the big back entrance to the Hall, the drive, part of the lawn, and the path leading to the stables and our drying ground; and then to the meadows and the river. This was a beautiful view of which I never tired, but sadly our ironing tables were under the other window and we could see only the courtyard and the kitchen. If there was the sound of horses' hooves then I would fly to the other window and crouch down to one side and watch.

There was a large octagonal closed stove towards the other end of the room, with room to walk all around it, and a pipe which went up towards the ceiling and then bent through the wall into the chimney. There were three ledges round this stove on which we placed our irons with their faces against the hot metal. We burnt coke in this, of course, and it sometimes burned so fiercely that the sides were red-hot. Then we had to damp it down; it was a great sin. My mother never taught me the "spit on the finger" method which most housewives used. We always tested the irons for heat against our faces. Constant use had burnished the bases of these irons like silver.

Behind this end wall was the airing room, which always had the most lovely smell of warmth, fresh grass and cleanliness — we laid household things on the grass to bleach when the weather was fit. There were hot pipes at floor level all round with shelves above, and the wall behind our big stove was warm too, and when on a Friday evening the shelves were stacked with beautifully laundered, sweet smelling linen, even a child who had had a part in it could get a sense of aesthetic satisfaction. On Saturday the washing was collected by the several people in charge, and we scrubbed the whole place down, and were generally away by about two o' clock. I was never able, then or since, to kneel down for any length of time without that horrible rising languor which ended in my keeling over, my face the colour of one of our sheets

CHAPTER
EIGHT

It was on our first Friday morning that Mrs Dawson paid us a visit. Although she had a housekeeper, she came in once a week to keep an eye on things, and to point out shortcomings, should she or anyone else have noticed any; one was never safe, really, at any time. That eye of hers, bulbous and protruding, could see through a brick wall, could see a flick of grime or a fly spot a mile off; and she loved catching any servant out "doing what she didn't oughter". So one always had to be prepared for her to come quietly in at the door under cover of the noise of the machines, and one could never know how long she had been watching, nor whether she had seen one slack off for that sinful moment, "wasting the time that she was paying for", when the floods of her most recent righteous wrath were loosed on one's head. At my first sight of her I decided that she was just like Mr Smith's turkey cock in a bad temper. She was short and fat but extremely well-corseted. The excess was mostly pushed up into bosom. Her face was bluish red, her eyes small but fierce and protruding, her nose beaky, and she had many chins; when she drew herself up to speak to us her breast puffed out, her chins grew red like wattles and she gobbled. She always looked as though there were an extremely bad smell under her nose. To my eternal shame, my Mother curtsied to her, but my knees, even under her compelling gaze, refused to bend. I only remember two of her remarks; "Well, Roberts, I expect you to know your duty and your position, and to keep to it". And of me, "She looks very thin." A lightning inspection revealed no immediate faults and she departed leaving Mother in no doubt as to the standard expected of us for fifteen shillings a week for two. She wore a lorgnette-cum-pince nez affair which was looped to the front of her dress somehow, and she always looked at one through it, which was most intimidating. She was the first person to call forth in me that personal pride which has perhaps been my besetting sin, and I can honestly recall that I was never servile to her though of course, I doubt if she ever spoke directly to me at all.

Colonel Dawson, a retired army man, large, with a blue face and large blue nose, easy going and now far too fond of the bottle and female servants, was completely managed by his wife. I should say she was of infinite value to him, looking after his interests completely, and ruling everyone with a rod of iron. The outside people showed a curious mixture of servility, in her presence, and sullen silence regarding her in her absence, unless they felt absolutely safe, when their remarks were far from polite; they were too afraid of losing their jobs and too mistrustful of each other, to say much. I remember later, when the Savilles were my friends, and there was an election pending, Mrs D had been round to each house telling each man for whom it was his duty to vote, and the inference was very plain. I had become politically minded by then, and was bitterly conscious of the fear and poverty around me, while being too ignorant to know that injustices and old ways could not be altered at the wave of a hat. I aired my views, of course, and they heard me silently. I could feel Mrs Saville willing her husband not to agree with me, fearing that I was too young to be discreet, but he only said quietly, with an intensity I have remembered, "Thank God there is a secret ballot." Then he said, "If only they could see what they are storing up for themselves." The writing was on the wall "for them to read, but they won't." I remember also when the Liberal Government brought in the "eightpence for fourpence Act", the footman came round to every servant with a petition against it which everyone had to sign, and did — us as well — though Mother and all the lower servants, who came in to talk to her as a respite from their duties when they could get away, had been jubilant about it. Every employee on the estate signed it too; the atmosphere was one of fear. Mr Saville had been a shepherd on the moor until the man at the Home Farm had had the temerity to ask for higher pay.

The Dawsons were too mean to employ a bailiff, preferring to pay a good man a working farmer's wage to do a working farmer's work and fit in most of a bailiff's duties as well. So this man was sacked and Saville promoted, and he knew quite well what would happen to him if he stepped out of line. Tom Train was waiting in his three-roomed cottage with his eight sickly children, and who could blame him for being eager to be a supplanter? The Dawsons, just before we went there, had changed from using a carriage and coachman to a fine new motor car, and a large, soft looking chauffeur drove them everywhere; but I heard mutters about the old coachman who, at the age of sixty, had been dismissed, just like that, after working on the estate since his youth. He was now living with a married daughter some way away, doing odd jobs with horses.

Weston is such a tiny place, I am always surprised to see it marked on the map. From the road between Otley and Ilkley you wouldn't see it, but of course it did possess a Hall, a Grange and a Manor. The Grange was at the end of the high stone wall that shut Weston Park off from the road, and was a small gracious place that I imagine must have been a Dower house — it belonged to the Hall — and its gardens had obviously been part of the Park. It was let to a wealthy young business man who went to Bradford each day, and his fashionably dressed snob of a wife was there all day with her two tiny children, nursemaid, two women maids and gardener, and I used to wonder whatever she did with herself all day long, for there was no kind of social life. Evaline's elder sister was the junior maid.

Next after the Grange stables, where the lane broke off from the road down to Weston Hall, was a small stone cottage occupied by the Head Keeper, nearing his nineties and a magnificent old man, still walking twelve miles or more a day with his gun under his arm.

86

A small village green was in front of this cottage, with an oak tree in the centre, a V.R. letter box on its trunk, and a complete pair of stocks in its shade; here we loved to sit on a summer evening, and Mr England would come out and sit and tell me about his son who had a thriving business somewhere not far off, of his other children who had all emigrated, and of his many grandchildren and great-grandchildren. And how lonely his poor old wife was all day long with no-one to go in and see her. I would like to be able to recall that as I grew older I did go in often but I am afraid my visits were most infrequent. The querulous complaints of an old woman are not much understood by the young.

On the other side of the road opposite the green were the gates of the Manor, much more ornate than the gates of the Hall, but the park was a long flat expanse of grass, very thinly wooded, with the house spread across in the distance; but I never went near the front of it so I have no memory of beauty or otherwise. The other thing I did love was a tiny copse just past the gate, which in early spring was white with the most wonderful snowdrops I have ever seen — I used to call them triple snowdrops. I had seen single ones before, and occasionally double ones in gardens, but these, growing apparently wild, outdid all others. They were followed by primroses and then bluebells, a flower hitherto unknown to me as it didn't grow at Felsted.

The people at the Manor were called Vavasour, and Evaline told me in great secrecy that they had a terrible quarrel with the Dawsons at the Hall. The families had been inseparable, and Miss Violet Vavasour, a haughty looking female I sometimes met out riding with a groom in attendance, had been engaged to Colonel Ashley, but it had been broken off. Evaline surmised her heart was broken too. Certainly there was no friendship now between the two houses, and bad blood between the servants on the rare occasions when they met. Col. Ashley was a cousin or something of the Dawsons and was frequently at the Hall, always in the company of the eldest daughter, riding with her round the countryside, so possibly she was something to do with the rift. Mrs Train hinted darkly, when I knew her better, that she was no better than she ought to be, but I thought she was a scraggy, long-nosed person with no looks at all, in spite of her fine clothes.

A spinney followed the lane for a couple of hundred yards after Mr England's cottage, and then our row of stone hovels started. The first one was occupied by the second gamekeeper, a large silent man with a silly, chattering wife and a tiny tubercular boy; then ours, then Train's, then the engineer's — an ex-naval man who drank secretly, though I have no idea how he got the liquor or the money to pay for it. He had two boys and a dirty, ragged wife who had been transplanted there from some dockside place like Liverpool, and who in her lonely misery occasionally broke out and rowed with him up and down the path outside — there wasn't room for her to express herself inside. The last old cottage housed a groom, but when he left and a footman wished to marry, he was allowed to bring his young wife there. After this a wide stretch of grass opened out, and along one side of this four newer cottages had been built, still in a terrace, but each with a good living room, largish, light kitchen with water and a sink and three bedrooms. The chauffeur had the first, the head gardener the second, but he had to house the under gardener, and the other two were let to outsiders. One was a horrible man called Dixon who was, I think, a commercial traveller from Leeds and only came home to his wife and family at weekends. In the last was the policeman who really operated from Otley, and covered a tremendous district on his bicycle.

In front of our old cottages was a path and then a beaten narrow strip of ground at the bottom of which were our two privies. Nowhere near any of the cottages was there a flower or any growing thing. Not even weeds grew, just the rough grass up at the top where we had a bonfire and swung our turnip lanterns on Bonfire Night. The pump was over the lane to the right of our cottage, and the farm gate about a hundred yards further down, and on that side fields stretched away into the distant hills. The lane meandered on, down through the woody tunnel to the back gate of the Hall. The woods ended here in pastures which led pleasantly to the river, and if one trod quietly and stood by the gate, the first field was alive with rabbits. It was fun to clap one's hands and watch the sea of bobbing white tails moving across, up the bank and into the shelter of the wood. But this wood had no flowers; it was a dark evil place to me, choked with dead wood, and dark rhododendron bushes pushing upwards trying to find the light.

Opposite the rabbit field were the stables, and after these the tiny church, almost hidden in rank grass. It was neglected beyond belief, unheated and uncleaned. The flagstones of the aisle were green with mould and fungus grew in the walls. There were two separate sorts of rooms, one each side of the aisle, for Hall servants and for the Family. The servants had hard chairs but the Family sat in armchairs with blue cushions with gold tassels, rather mouldy and tarnished now. Here the men used to snooze while the lady kept her eye on the servants. In the churchyard, nearly hidden by rank grass, was a stone door leading to a vault where generations of Dawsons slept, the ladies' eyes now mercifully closed forever.

The living to this church was in the gift of the Dawsons, but the latest incumbent, who had been there some years, was a spiritualist, and as such repugnant to Mrs Dawson who fought to have him turned out, but the Bishop would not consent. So Mr Tweedale stayed, and was boycotted. He was an extraordinary figure, wearing the clothes of his early manhood, a wide black cloak down to his heels, and a low top hat, very dull, with a curly brim. I know I thought he looked like the Devil, and would not have been surprised if he had vanished in a puff of smoke, or a tail with a fork had appeared below the cloak. He took no notice whatever of any of us, just stalked in, did his little piece and stalked out again, up the hill and through the village and never spoke nor was spoken to.

I "took over" this church in earlyish days. Though there was no congregation save one man who walked about a mile every Sunday evening to hear the sermon — for Mr Tweedale, when he did preach, did so very well — a youth of fifteen, Harry, came out from Otley twice every Sunday to play the American organ; he was a poor boy whose ambition it was to be an organist. I had started going, and sang the hymns with gusto, and soon Harry asked me if I could get any more girls to come and make a choir. Evaline could not come because the Dawsons would have objected, and anyhow they were Chapel, but the three Dixon girls came, one from the Manor cottages, and Harry brought a boy friend of his, and the six of us sang the hymns and responses very happily. Mr Tweedale would sometimes go off into a sort of trance in the middle of the service and start communing with "something" at the rear of the church, and the backs of our necks would start tingling with pleasurable anticipation, but nothing ever materialised, and then came his usual formula, "As there are not more than three adults in the congregation there will be no sermon", so we sang a last hymn and he went home. But we always stayed our full time and practised anthems from books Harry had brought. For some reason at Harvest Festival time, people would come out from Otley for a service and pack the little church, and singing friends of Harry's came and made a real choir, and in my second year we sang an anthem "The valleys stand so thick with corn", and I had a two-line solo and nearly burst with pride. Mr Tweedale preached a Harvest sermon and didn't mention spirits once and there was a bumper collection.

Mrs Tweedale always seemed a most pathetic figure to me. She was obviously a lady, and Mrs Train had a story that she was not married to Mr Tweedale but had run away from her husband to be with him. She also wore outlandish clothes, long and very full skirts with trains, and a fur cape and hats that were not at all like those that other people wore. She had an awful time at the Rectory because they had very little money, and could only get the youngest, cheapest servants, and she had three children. They were educated at home until they were quite big, and then the authorities said they must go to school, so they came along to the village school and were very clever children indeed.

From December to March I was a laundry maid, working from six in the morning till six at night, stumbling with my mother up the hill in the dark, tired out, and ready for sleep after making our bed and tidying up the little place and helping to prepare a meal. It was a shocking little cottage, just one room up and one down with a stone cellar underground, to which one stumbled down a spiral of stone steps; Mother insisted that bread and milk had to be kept down there. As it was infested with beetles, on more than one occasion we cut a loaf which proved to be a mere shell full of the horrible things, and it was not easy either, to negotiate those steps with a candle in one hand and a jug of milk in the other. There was a small cupboard in our room for storage and a space under the stairs for coal.

Some time at the end of March I fell down the stone stairs from the ironing room, carrying a "pot" bowl of water with which I had been doing some cleaning, and sustained a broken elbow. I remember I thrust it into the bend of the stairs as I fell in an effort not to break the bowl, which of course shattered. As Mother picked me up I sobbed in real terror of her anger that the bowl was broken, to which to my astonishment she said, "Damn the bowl". The doctor was sent for — to my relief Mrs Dawson was not at home — my arm was strapped up, the housekeeper sent me hot tea, and I spent the rest of the day in a chair by the hot stove. But the cat was out of the bag, for the doctor made it his business to tell Mrs Dawson that I was a child of twelve and should be at school until I was fourteen. I think if it had been easy to get laundry maids in that place, Mother would have been sent away, but it just happened that Dith was being sent home in disgrace, having been out in a boat with the boys at the vicarage when she ought to have been doing housework, so Mrs D. said she would see if she would "do". She did not do, and Doff was sent for, and came and took my place, and Dith went away to another situation. Poor Doff, to be back in thrall again; I know she felt it was all my fault. Though she had been working in a laundry as a maid, there were nice married couples around who had seen how sweet she was and been really kind to her; she had done what had obviously been her intention on getting away from Mother and attended evening classes in Redhill to make up for her lost education. And now it had to stop, and I knew she was in despair.

The elbow proved troublesome, it had broken awkwardly, and also the doctor said to Mother, "This girl is very ricketty", but a month of no laundry work and my days to myself were a marvellous tonic. I did what I could at home, and then with my dinner in a bit of newspaper spent the daylight hours exploring; the park first, miles of it all to myself. On the hilly side, the road bridged a rocky little beck which danced through a grey stone arch and fell in little cascades down the hill, turning corners out of sight, reappearing demurely further on at a gentle pace on its way to the river. I walked through the avenue of trees and came upon the Banqueting Hall, an ancient and beautiful place. I pushed the door gingerly and it opened. The present owners, while preserving its outward beauty had constructed a swimming pool inside, with a big playroom at one end. There was a billiard table — which I did not recognise — and lots of gun apparatus and fishing rods in cases and on the walls. All round the walls were glass-fronted cupboards with treasures which the children had garnered over many happy childhood years — collections of birds' eggs, stuffed birds and fishes, coloured stones and pieces of rock, everything labelled with the boy's name and when and where it was caught or found. And books of foreign stamps and pressed flowers — I remember that it hit me like a blow that there existed children so cherished that all the joys of their childhood should have been collected and, as it were, embalmed here.

Yet I was very happy about the place and visited it many times, and I do not know to this day why I was not ordered away, for I did with the whole of Weston Park what I had done with Mr Smith's fields, I took possession of it. It was mine, and my private life and my fantasies were all set in it. Only once was I surprised there, much later. Mr Crust, the valet approached, stiff as a ramrod, from one direction, as I from the other, and as I stood poised for flight, asked me kindly if I would like to go in with him. I dared not tell him how familiar I was already with the place so was shown round and told of how Master Stopham had caught that fish, and with what bait, and Master Jack shot that bird on the wing when he was only twelve with one bullet from his airgun — loving, proud reminiscences of two boys to whom he had given many years of his life. Captain Stopham Dawson was with his regiment in England, and very often at home, and I could not reconcile the boy of these stories with the handsome, arrogant man who strode about with Cole, the Second Keeper, his gun under his arm, as if he owned the world — as of course he did, this part of it. Master Jack was with his regiment in India, Miss Kitty I have mentioned, and the youngest, Miss Phyllis, who was about a year older than me, very much an afterthought, went to school in Bradford. She was a weekly boarder, taken and fetched by car. I despised her cheerfully, while not knowing her at all. She was large and fat and very plain, and — I decided — stupid, with a mane of coarse, thick mouse-coloured hair in a heavy plait. I had never liked my own hair much — it was fine and straw coloured and curling and unkempt — but I preferred it to hers.

The Banqueting Hall was set among the trees and hills back from the big drive, but where this curved right, a smaller path wandered down to a huge lake. The banks on one side of its perimeter were lush grass with flags and forget-me-nots and milkmaids and all kinds of reeds and water plants. But between it and the house were close-shaven lawns like light green silk. The great house spread across a wide expanse, and was gracious and lovely. No trees or bushes shut off its view across the green and the blue and the park stretching away, though there were low growing flowers in beds, and it was flanked by flowering shrubs and some exotic looking trees. I decided later the house was Queen Anne, grey stone, long and fairly low with a balustrade along the top and tall windows. I knew nothing of architecture of course, but it satisfied my eye. The drive curled up and round the lawns, one branch disappearing through the trees to the back of the house, the other going along the front to the great door with its curved stone steps, tall columns and portico.

I found my way to the river, and was so enchanted that I went there day after day. The Wharfe was broad as it flowed through Weston grounds, and clear as crystal, with a stony rock bed, a real trout river, Mr Crust told me. The first time I went there I found the boat. It was tied up about half a mile away, and by dint of much tugging and water over my boots, I dragged it near enough to get in. There was water in the bottom, of course, but that didn't worry me, and for a couple of days I didn't go much further. Then I took off my boots and stockings and with my skirts tucked up round my middle I paddled in the water, icy in the deeper places but soft and warm in the shallows, watching the play of light over the stones, the different colours of the water-washed pebbles, the sudden "whoosh" as a water bird flew at my approach, its wings beating and feet trailing ripples on the surface. Then I would sit in the boat in the sun — it must have been a fine April that year — and watch the fish rise to flies, and little fluffy water animals hurry about their business.

Soon I was exploring further, and round a bend came suddenly on what could have been serious for me. The banks had been getting rougher and higher with rocky hillocks leading back, and here was quite a sizeable waterfall galloping down to my left side. In my open-mouthed, gaping admiration of its beauty I stepped off my shallower course into cold, deeper water from the fall up to my middle. My left arm was in a sling, of course, but somehow I struggled back by hanging onto low-growing vegetation overhanging the water, but I was desperately frightened, for the fall had quite a menacing roar, and just there round the bend the sun was shut away. I struggled over to the gentler bank, and back to the sunshine to dry. And I had my reward. When I did amble on again, on the inside of the bend, rising ground began to be clothed in bracken and silver birch trees, and suddenly on the slope unrolled a rising carpet of blue. These were my first bluebells. Had I seen a few, I would have thought them beautiful, but to see them for the first time in this profusion, this prodigality, bemused my senses. I sat on a fallen log and looked, and looked, and soaked in the sight of the rising slopes of deep blue, misting almost to grey crowned with the tender young green and silver of the birches, spreading along the river as far as I could see. I remember the way home seemed very long. I was tired out and almost drunk with beauty, but I have carried the picture of that scene with me for over fifty years.

CHAPTER
NINE

The school was at Askwith, a mile and a half away, and six or so assorted children walked there in all weathers, in thick dust, deep mud, snow almost to our knees, often arriving soaked to the skin. The winding road led over our stream and down the banks which fell away on either side with a carpet of flowers most of the year, and the scents of violets, primroses and then wild mint rose like incense to our fresh, young noses. There were always birds' nests in the lane and we watched them jealously and cried our hearts out when one of the boys found the nests later and scattered the fledglings on the ground while the parents beat about piteously.

I started school on Mayday. My arm had been bent into position and bound up with a sort of sticky brown bandage, which set stiff, and was left for quite a while. Then it was ripped off and another one put on, and made immovable to my side. However, now they were off altogether, and my squashed-looking arm had to be exercised every day to get the use back into it, and I had to wear a sling, which made me feel important. I wasn't very good at seeing to it myself though, and it was rather a mess. Sadly, too, I had lost my pink striped uniform, and had outgrown what clothes I had.

Mysteriously, the nice ladies' maid brought two charming flowered blouses and a gymslip of navy blue which Miss Phyllis had outgrown. However, Mother said they were for Sundays, so I went to school with neat little Evaline, looking like nothing on earth and was definitely not a success. No-one in Askwith or Weston had much money, except perhaps a farmer or two, but nearly every child was clean and neat — and small. I may have been fairly clean by then, but I was certainly not neat. My skirts hung in loops round my ankles — though I had a clean pinafore over the top — I wore shoes that were not bought for me in summer, and hobnailed boots in winter, and as we had no mirror, my hair was probably parted in all the wrong places. I topped every girl in school bar one, and most of the boys, by a head. I had longed for school like a stream of water in a thirsty land, as the psalmist says, but Mrs Brown, the Mistress, and I detested each other on sight. I honestly think that from the first she set out to humiliate me.

There were about sixty children of all ages in the school then, with two teachers. The building was new, only two years old, one long room with a movable partition dividing the infants from the older children. Although on being asked, I told her I had been for some time in the top class at Felsted, she put me with little girls of ten and eleven at first, but at a table by myself, where I felt like Gulliver among the Lilliputians or Alice among the little animals. When she found that I had indeed gone much further in all subjects than she taught but was shockingly untidy, she set me to

100

copy-writing for hours on end, starting with pothooks, and going very gradually upwards. She herself was an exquisite writer, in the fashion of the early Victorian period, and actually made the children practise this style, small and fat like herself, with all sorts of squiggles coming out of the letters, and with the capitals at the beginning of paragraphs decorated with different coloured inks. For hours we would sit practising this, and the best would go up on the wall.

Mrs Brown was about fifty, an ignorant uncertificated teacher, married to a Baptist minister who lived away somewhere and only saw his family at intervals. She had a boy and girl at the school, two ginger-haired, sneaky little prigs who were favoured above others all the time, and a nice boy of about sixteen at home, who was supposed to be studying, but was in reality the maid of all work, who cleaned and cooked for them all. The women in the village spoke fair to Mrs Brown's face, but said a lot of things behind her back that would have made her gingery hair stand on end. She liked to think of herself as a power in the place, for there was no communal life at all, only a chapel in a barn, and they had only local preachers.

Her knowledge of arithmetic was quite rudimentary; she gave me cards to work from by myself, so I never did get any further than simple decimals and fractions. I never had a book so I could tackle anything more complicated. We did the same history as at Felsted, Alfred, and the Conqueror, and Victoria in her nightgown and shawl thrown in for good measure. She had a way, when she was not very well-up in a subject, of wandering off into reminiscences. An English geography lesson would remind her of a holiday in Blackpool, while anything further afield would recall a friend who went to Australia or some such place. She made a letter from a friend who was a missionary somewhere the starting point for lessons on several subjects, which all slid off into cosy talks about the friend's good family and beautiful nature and personal appearance. We also heard how much the friend owed to Mrs Brown's example, which had encouraged her to venture into far away places, spreading the light to the heathen. Mrs Brown was horribly "pi" but had no real Christianity at all. Christ himself would have offended her sense of propriety.

She was also a coward and a bully. She would nag the young teacher under her, and not uphold her authority; of course the children took advantage. Once a new young girl, trying to impose discipline, slapped a small boy who was rude to her; at dinner time his big brother and about five mates came into where we were eating and started a rough house. She was only about seventeen, I think, and stood up to them, but they banged her with exercise books and her hair fell down, and we, cowards that we were, made no attempt to help her when they tipped her chair over and she fell to the floor. When she ran out into the playground they followed and made her fall again, and all this with horrible abuse. Mrs Brown appeared then, in time to see her pick herself up and to hear her shouting in anger at the boys, and was immediately horrified at such unladylike behaviour — no teacher should speak so. She would listen to nothing the poor girl said. Mrs Brown was astounded that a teacher of hers could so far forget herself as to speak so to children; when we were appealed to, to give evidence as to the boys' attack, we were shooed away and told it would all have to be gone into. But it wasn't. Mrs Brown after due consideration gave the poor girl one of her lectures in front of the whole school, pointing out the evils of losing one's self control, when the poor girl lost hers properly and raved so at Mrs Brown that that lady called on the boys to protect her, and the girl ran out and never came back again. Her father did, but Mrs Brown could always lie her way out of any situation. Another day, the boiler went wrong, the pipes began to bump and hiss, and the small children began to cry. Her desk was near the door, and calling the infant teacher to line everyone up in order so there should be no panic, she courageously led the children out into the playground, leaving the student teacher to bring up the rear.

My drawing was no help to me here for girls were not allowed to draw, only boys did that. Girls had to paint flowers, using a puddle of watercolour in a little bowl, and making blobs with a brush, forming them into the shape of a daisy. I always took far too much liquid on my brush and made ghastly messes, unless I cheated and drew my flower with the tip of the brush, and then filled in the outline. This was definitely not allowed; it was not "painting". Mrs Brown did appreciate English though, and in spite of herself had to give me credit for a gift in that direction. She would read out loud and "tut tut" over my poems and compositions, and say "Now where did she get that from, I wonder?" till I could have hit her. She had this way of talking "at" me through the others which was infuriating.

We children from Weston, about six of us, had to take our dinners each day, as school was a mile and a half from home. Evaline had a wicker basket with two little sloping half lids, and her mother packed her meal exquisitely — a meat pasty, some bread and butter cut thinly, with jam, a couple of cakes, and always a bottle of milk, all neatly covered by a napkin. I had thick bread and maybe cheese, sometimes meat, in newspaper. We all had to eat in the infants' room, even in summer when we would have preferred to have eaten outside; but in cold weather we sat by the warm stove. Here I found a joy which affected me lastingly — a piano. I had never come near to one before, and found to my joy that I could play by ear. It is extraordinary now to remember how little music was heard by people away from towns early in the century, and to find that I could play any song I knew was magic. I also saw printed music for the first time, for the infant teacher had to play marches and songs, and there was always something in the piano. I pestered Evaline, who had lessons on their harmonium, to tell me the letters of the notes of the scale — I knew tonic solfa, having learned from the chart at Felsted where I was always given a tonic copy of the music to help the others learn the songs. With a sixpence acquired goodness knows how, I bought a copy of Ezra Read's *Piano Tutor*, and soon

104

knew more than Evaline. I smile when I think of all this. I cut up a long cardboard box, and made a semblance of a keyboard — there was a long paper one folded into the cover of the *Piano Tutor* — and cut the white notes so they would depress a little under my fingers. I couldn't cut the black ones but could only block them in, and I only had room for two octaves, but on this I got the notes of the scale and their position on the keyboard firmly fixed.

Then later on I won a shilling in a race and bought a toy piano painted white, with flowers on it. This had two octaves too, and with this and my *Piano Tutor* I managed to acquire a considerable knowledge of simple music. Once I got going, I read music at sight and in my later life, mixing with the best amateur singers and many professionals, met few who could read better than I. Mrs Brown graciously found my singing of use too, and when in a good mood, and having other work to do, would give me a song to teach to a younger class. I used to feel awful, out in front in all my untidiness, and she used to look me up and down in a far from kind way.

At some time I became aware that the school was beginning to practise for an annual concert. At first, apparently, I was to be left out, but she had to keep bringing me in. We were learning songs and sketches — dreadfully feeble things — and stomping round the classroom with hoops of paper flowers, and those children were such duffers! They couldn't learn poems or songs without dreadful stumbles. There was a great deal of whispering about clothes and new dresses, and I stayed stonily outside, but one day a miracle happened. A note had been sent to my mother, and she and Doff dug out of the hamper a piece of blue serge, and someone gave some blue silk, and the dressmaker in Askwith made me a new dress. In Mother's curious way, she didn't tell me, just gave me a parcel and told me to call on Mrs Smith. And when Mrs Smith pleasantly and importantly told me to take my dress off to be measured I could have fallen through the floor, for my underclothes were in their usual state of incorrectness and disrepair, and I was very conscious of the fact that I hadn't had an all-over wash since I left the laundry. Still, she made me a charming dress in which I felt like a fairy princess, and even Mrs Brown approved. I found on "the night" that all the other big girls had white dresses, but even this did not dim my radiance a bit.

The schoolroom was packed on the evening and the school governors were there. I was supposed to appear only once, to recite a poem I had written which had been praised by a visiting inspector; but they couldn't sing their songs without me. There was a silly sketch about "being sunbeams", in which a boy of thirteen had to sing "If I were a sunbeam, I know what I would do," and he could not remember the words or sing in tune; so he had to turn his back on the audience while I sang "off". Then the answering angel tripped on, her arms hung with muslin wings — she was the only girl taller than me, but the daughter of a farmer and very much to be considered — and she could not pronounce a squeak either, so I sang her verse hidden behind her.

Poor Evaline had been going to sing but had been taken ill with pneumonia, so I had to sing her song, which I knew from helping her learn it, so that was no hardship. The difficulty was getting a costume at short notice, for hers would never fit me. The song was supposed to be sung by an elegant unmarried lady, bemoaning the passing of the days "when I was a girl, you know"; but they fixed me up with a black silk skirt with a bustle, and a sealskin cape, and a poke bonnet and a reticule. I really could sing well for a youngster, and brought the house down. I was most highly commended in the Otley newspaper and with the grown-ups at least was never looked down on quite so much afterwards. And my poem was printed in full too, with remarks from Mrs Brown that it had been inspired by one of her geography lessons.

The next week one of the school governors came to school, and after conferring with Mrs Brown called me out to talk to him. I felt awful and I expect I sounded and looked so, but he asked me how I would like to go away to a good school to be educated. Of course I didn't say it was the dream of my life. All I could say, taken by surprise, was the one thing I knew, that I would not be allowed to go; so he said, "Well, we will see." I went back to my seat with my head in the clouds, but feeling that my middle had dropped through my boots, and only a misty sort of bit of me was left. Mrs Brown came over afterwards and said Mr Walker had left it to her to sound out my mother, and discuss the possibilities. Would Mother go and see her? She said she hoped I realised what they were trying to do for me, but from the way she looked down her nose I knew I could not expect much help from her. The school he had in mind was the one Miss Phyllis attended, and at home in the evening I tried to tell Mother and Doff about it. Doff shut up like a clamp and Mother said, "Oh, so you've started, have you?" and that was that. Curiously, Mother did go to see Mrs Brown, but I was never told what transpired. For myself, I was so mixed up; I dreamed of going away to another institution, but one where I would learn all the lovely things there were in the world to be learnt, but I saw myself in my awful clothes among the other girls, and Miss Phyllis there too, and I just knew it couldn't happen. However, it was all soon over.

Mrs Brown had an obsession about sex. You could never start squashing the dreadful thing too early. Boys were boys and girls were girls, and should be kept in absolutely separate pens, so though we were a small mixed school we were segregated. Both in the classrooms and the playground there was an invisible line over which you strayed at your peril, but of course this could not apply off the school premises. It was the "top" season, and the boys who could afford them bought tops at the little village shop, and those who couldn't made them by whittling down cotton reels and hammering a rounded hob-nail into the pointed end. I made myself one, and soon a number of girls did the same, and boys and girls together played tops on a piece of smooth ground outside the chapel before we Weston children went home after school. But not for long! When we went into the classroom one morning,

Mrs Brown said in a voice of doom, she wanted these girls to stand out at the back of the class where she could see them: me, and Evaline and Nora Middlemass and Madge — the pretty favourite — and a couple of others, about all the biggest girls. She said she had seen a dreadful thing, a thing that could not have happened before the coming of the strangers into their midst, but her girls, on the training of whom she had spent so much time and thought — they were all in tears by now — led by this stranger, had been playing "tops" in the street, bending over and — here she lowered her eyes — displaying their underwear in the presence of the other sex (in a hushed whisper). She blethered on for some minutes until most of the children were weeping, but I, not knowing what all the fuss was about, yet realising I was the villain of the piece, merely looked mulish and sullen. She wound up with an appeal to "her" girls to return to their ladylike ways, and to me, the venomous remark; "As for you, I cannot turn you from your wicked ways, but I can see that you do not go where you can affect others." And she did, and that was that.

But the killing of the dream which, in spite of myself, had woken inside me, hardened me in some way, and when some months later Mrs Brown was leaving and the girls were weeping hypocritical tears with her at the thought of her going, I did not join in. She said, "You are glad I am going, aren't you?" and I said, "Yes, I am." I think I would normally only say something unkind in the heat of the moment, but that time I felt coldly cruel.

Miss Tinniswood, the new headmistress, was as intelligent as Mrs Brown was stupid. She was tall, with a sallow, thin face and dark humorous eyes. She came from a town, prepared to love the country and country children, but of course, she was a "foreigner", and as such the children treated her in school, as their parents did out of school, with sullenness and outright rudeness. I sat there and loved her, but she wasn't to know that a rough-looking lump like me was any different from the others; and for a week or two they gave her a terrible time. But she was obviously an old campaigner, and one morning turned up with a tough cane, which she laid on her desk. She went halfway through the morning until they had forgotten the cane and began to vie with each other in impudence, and when one big boy left his desk and approached her with some yokel impudence or other, she snatched it up and brought it down round his shoulders with such force that he howled. She followed it immediately with another; the hubbub died at once. This was the kind of discipline they understood, and while the boy stood and rubbed himself, she went back to her desk. She was obviously fighting with tears, but kept them back, and then she talked. She said she had come there to teach them, and they badly needed teaching, and not they nor their parents would drive her away. She did not want to use the cane, but if she had to, she would. That was all; no interminable, wordy lectures, no appeals to them to behave like little ladies and gentlemen, but she had got through to them, and after that did not have much trouble.

Thank goodness, soon she found how much I needed her and became a real friend to me. I had had no books to read since Felsted, and she lent me all she had that I had not read — especially poetry: Longfellow, Shelley, Coleridge, Tennyson and Milton. Also from her, I learned to write. She didn't try to teach me, but I copied her style, a plain, even, flowing writing with no ornamentation, and it suited me, and all my life since I have been accounted a good writer. I went to see Miss Tinniswood later on, when I was leaving the district, and she was very happy and successful with the children. The big ones of my time had left, of course, but the young ones were brighter and more responsive already. She was very grieved about the white-faced, hollow-eyed, spindle-legged tubercular children — there was quite a spattering of them — and she said there were quite as many in proportion in that village as in the poor parts of the town she had come from, and these were not necessarily from the poorest homes, either. She said goodbye to me fondly, and said, "Whatever you do or do not do, remember you must write, and keep on writing." But I didn't.

CHAPTER
TEN

During this time when I was at school we lost three little boys at Weston with TB: Dickie Cole the lusty great gamekeeper's child, Charlie Clarkson the gardener's son, and poor little Jackie Train. Jackie was eleven when he died, and had lain in a little box cupboard of a room since he was four with a TB hip. The doctor rode out from Otley most weeks to see him, and Mrs Dawson sent flowers and toys, but I suppose in those days there was no cure or alleviation for such unfortunates. I heard a lot about Jackie but knew nothing about real sickness, and one day coming back from my wanderings laden with flowers, took a bunch to Mrs Train's door and asked her if Jackie would like them. I didn't know if she would be pleased, for she was not at all outgoing, but to my surprise she was delighted and said would I take them up to him myself. "Oor Jackie" had heard a lot about me and would like to see me. Not thinking, I followed her up the narrow twisting stairs to the half floor, but when she stood aside for me to enter the room I nearly fell down them again with fright, for there on the white pillow in the little bed, surrounded by hothouse flowers, was a grey-white little death's head, eyes sunken right in their sockets, and the ghastly mouth with broken off, rotting teeth, grinning at me. I hadn't the wit not to show my horror, and caused the poor mother some distress, I fear, but when the little fellow spoke to me and thanked me for coming I managed to pull myself together and sit by the bed, and talk to him about the fields where I had picked the flowers, and the river I loved, which, as he whispered, he had never seen. He had picture books, but could not read. His mother didn't leave me long, and as I stumbled out again she said that I mustn't mind his looks, poor lad, it had done him so much good to see someone.

I made a vow to myself that I would see him once a week, but I was not a sufficiently thoughtful girl to keep it, besides which, the skull amid the bright flowers haunted me, and though I felt pity, I also felt fear and revulsion. I think I did go in twice, and then later that summer, Jackie died. The little coffin was pushed down the hill to the church on a handcart from the farm, and only Mr and Mrs Train and the engineer's wife followed it. Hilda, the eldest girl, came home to be with the children. Those little ones were laid in the earth with the minimum of fuss and expense, and in a few weeks the rough grass and weeds hid the small mounds, and only in the poor mothers' hearts was there a permanent memorial.

The only other occasion when I knew the church to be used other than on Sundays, was when Alice Crabtree from "oop on't moor" had to get married. Mr Crabtree was a respectable farmer living about a mile from the shepherd's cottage where Mrs Saville had gone as a bride, and where her children had been born. Mrs Crabtree was then her near neighbour, and they passed the time of day when they met, but women of their type did not call each other "friends". They had no room for anything in their lives but their husbands and families, and were content to respect other people of whom they approved. Both families were ardent "chapel", narrow and intolerant. When Mrs Crabtree found that Alice, their pretty eldest daughter, and the apple of her father's eye, was going to have a baby by a gawky young clodhopper who worked on the farm, she walked all of six miles down to Weston to Mrs Saville, and poured it out to her. To both of these women the young people had committed the unforgivable sin — the "scarlet woman" loomed large in their religion — but there was no comfort there for her. The inexorable law for women — how often I heard it made to fit any marital discomfort — was "she's made her bed, now she must lie on it". And that was definitely Mrs Saville's dictum. Poor Mrs Crabtree, I suppose the taking of some action was a relief to her, just to share her grief with someone who would understand it, for she knew her husband wouldn't. When he knew he set his face hard, turned his young daughter out of doors, the boy out of his job, and wiped them out of his life. The mother insisted they must marry, so Weston church was the only place for the sorry job. I saw them as they tramped up the hill again through the woody tunnel, two giggling adolescents, the girl big already — the first time I had noticed such a thing, but Evaline had told me about them and I looked for it. Mrs

114

Crabtree, in tears, and her next eldest girl with her were the only ones who attended. Mrs Saville's door remained closed.

There was another case where this hardness of the women became very apparent to me. The young man who was now shepherd on the Moor was a fine, yellow-haired, handsome fellow, a devil with the girls. He had married a young woman whose father kept a prosperous pub miles away somewhere, and brought her straight from her father's bar, where she had been the centre of attraction, to a lonely moorland cottage with no neighbour nearer than a mile, and those neighbours the Crabtrees. She went nearly wild with loneliness. It was not quite so bad at first for she could walk down with him to the "Bull" at Askwith, but when her baby was coming and she began to get querulous, he lost his caring for her and went off by himself. She started walking down to Weston, for after all he worked for the Dawsons, but got short shrift from Mrs Saville, who told her bluntly to go home where she belonged. When her baby came, Mrs Saville told Evaline and me to take up a basket of good home food for her, for as she said, "She's a poor thing, and won't have provided." She was so glad to see us she cried all over us, as Evaline said contemptuously.

Whereas the shepherd's wife looked upon the cottage as the veriest hovel, to Evaline it was a shrine of happy memories, and every stone was dear to her; she showed me where she and Frank had done this or that and the bedroom she had shared with Alice, and the patch in the garden that had been her own — the garden was

115

now quite untended. And at the farm the big old fireplace in the living room, with the bread oven at the side. Evaline said there was nothing like it at the farm for comfort or for cooking. She implored us to visit her again, but of course we didn't and so she started dragging herself down to Weston about once a week, with the baby in a terrible old pram, hanging round the cottages trying to talk to the women, and waiting about for Evaline or me, and she used to rave about her husband and all his unkindness and infidelity. That didn't suit the women. Whatever your husband did, you straightened it out yourself. It was up to you to "best" him. If you didn't, so much the worse for you. Life had made these women tough. In the end, after threatening suicide all over the place, she somehow made her way home to her father, and we did not see her again. And I have no memory of her name.

Although Edith was not now at home to take all Doff's affection, she still had not much time for me. After working a twelve-hour day she still studied hard and tramped three evenings a week into Otley to evening classes. I adored her, and would plead with her to come for walks with me at weekends. Once she said she would, and we planned to picnic on the Chevin. The day was fine, and then she said that Evaline could come too, for Evaline also thought she was wonderful, and when we started off I was so proud and happy. But Doff talked to Evaline and made a fuss of Evaline, just like she used to of Dith, and they took no notice of me. I tagged along, and a black despair took possession of me, crept all over into my heart and my stomach and my head and made it ache, and sat on my chest and oppressed me, and then on top of the Chevin they laughed at me because I wouldn't join in when they teased me, and once again the world seemed a dreadful place. All the way home I wept intensely, inwardly.

Curious that a child who had been such a "sniveller" should grow into someone who found tears almost impossible outwardly. Quick annoyances have always brought tears to my eyes, but all real grief has seemed to sear my whole body, and dry up the wells that might bring relief. In the same way I have never been able to fly into a temper when hurt and so clear out the vapours of annoyance or misunderstanding with a good explosion. The words spring to my lips, but something holds them back, just like the vomit in the bus that time, and then it goes sour on me, instead of leaving me empty but clean. I remember often being battered with hard words that stunned my mind, and then the batterer not being able to understand why I could not be happy again when it was all over. I suppose temper is a safety valve and mine had got blocked up.

Doff and Mother went to London from Weston twice for a weekend. The first time was not long after I went to school. I was not on visiting terms with the Savilles yet but friendly with the Dixon girls, and I was allowed to ask if Phyllis, the middle one, could come and stay with me; but Mrs Dixon said "No", I could stay with them, and I was very excited. But it did not happen, because Mr Dixon made one of his periodic visits home that weekend bringing a fluffy-looking woman with him. They came on Friday, and on Saturday morning

Mrs Dixon took him up a cup of tea and found the fluffy woman in bed with him in the place she had vacated. Although Mrs Dixon was a mild, sweet woman, she was not pleased and Phyllis came down to me, told me all about it, and said she was staying with me after all. We had sausages for dinner for a treat, and I dropped the pan of hot fat on Phyllis's foot and she had a very nasty place. Also the tale of Mr Dixon and his fluffy woman got all round the cottages and I was blamed, so I was not popular with Mrs Dixon for a while, though I had not said a word. I was not on gossiping terms with anyone, and anyhow did not understand the significance of what had happened. The next time they went to London, a year later, it was lovely. Mrs Saville invited me to stay with them, and as Mother left on Friday, because the Dawsons were away, I had two whole days of bliss. In my eyes then the farm and house were wonderful.

The square four-up four-down farmhouse was built off the road on the side of the hill, just before it began its steepest descent through the woody tunnel. Though the back was well below ground level, the front sat high and wide and smiling facing the flower garden which was Mrs Saville's pride and joy. An orchard was on the opposite side from the road, then the farmyard with huge great buildings, larger than anything Mr Smith had had; haylofts and granaries and cart and implement sheds, but all very private and workmanlike. No nice duck pond and winding stream, but cats and kittens by the dozen.

You went to the house through the back gate from the road, into a smallish yard where the pigsties were. The pigs were colossally fat and stood up to their bellies in the muck, sticking out their bottom lips and watching out of their wicked little eyes until their food came. Then they would be at the trough squealing and fighting before the man could pour it out, and he had to keep pushing them away with his foot. The back door to the farmhouse was over the other side of the yard, but not far away. You went down steps into the back kitchen, where all the preparation of food and washing up was done, but just across the yard opposite this door was the bakehouse, where Mrs Saville washed clothes and did the main cooking, and sometimes there was a great deal of this, for the horseman and the casual Irish workers who came each year for the different seasons had to be looked after by Mrs Saville. A hundred times a day, she could go backwards and forwards from the back kitchen to the bakehouse, and the bakehouse to the kitchen, her wooden pattens clacking, with a woollen comforter on her head and a knitted bodice affair with long ends crossed over her front and tied behind. The men sat here in the evenings when they were not working, but at other times it was a cosy haven of warmth for us to be alone in. We used to bake potatoes in the ashes under the bottom grid of the fire. The great wide stove was shining with black lead and elbow grease, with every possible point picked out in a highlight of polished steel. It had to be done every day with emery paper to keep it so, I well know.

On the other side of the back door was the dairy. You went through a door from the back kitchen and down steps to it. It was all stone, with whitewashed walls so thick that the temperature seemed the same all year. There was a wide stone shelf, waist high, on each side, and on each shelf stood five or six glass pancheons, shallow, narrow at the bottom but widening out to about three feet across the top. Mrs Saville said they had been there "'underds of 'ears". I asked, whatever would happen if she broke one, and she said, "Eh lass, don't think on such things. It 'ud be more 'n our job were worth." Each bowl was full of milk, and she made pounds and pounds of butter a week, and what was not used at the Hall was sold, and of course we all bought skimmed milk at a penny a jug. The butter churn was of wood, whitey-yellow with scrubbing, and the picture in my mind, of white walls and greenish gleam of old glass, yellow cream and red brick floor, shining utensils hanging on the walls, is of a lovely part of English life that has gone forever.

Yet what work there was! Mrs Saville never stopped, yet I never knew a woman more truly happy with her state of life than she was. Also, she is the only woman who ever spoke to me of the love of a husband being the one essential for a woman's happiness. "Thee'll get thee a man, lass," she would say, "Niver fear, and thee own little place, and thee'll love'im, and the childer'll come, and thee'll have all thee wants and be 'appy." Hers was a very simple philosophy. She called her husband "Measter" and could scarcely read, yet kept her accounts impeccably for Mrs Dawson, in a stroke and cross system of her own. She never left the farm except once every Sunday, wet or fine, to go to chapel in Askwith. It made me smile to see them for they walked in single file, like ducks going to water; Mr Saville first, then his wife, then Alice, then Evaline. The only deviation was when Frank was home for the day, when he walked with his father.

For the rest, the large kitchen, which would now be called the living room, was nearly half of the front of the house, and the "Room" was the other half, intersected by the narrow passage leading from the front door to the stairs which went straight up to a square landing from which the bedroom doors opened. I slept with Evaline in her big bed, sinking deep into the feathers, and never had I seen, let alone shared, such luxury. We at home slept three in a bed in a little room with no other furniture in it. Evaline had this large room to herself, her bed had two great, fat, fluffy pillows with frilled pillowcases, lovely white sheets and a white honeycomb quilt all smelling of lavender; and she had a polished chest of drawers with her underclothes in and a press against the wall for her other clothes; and a great drawer full of blankets underneath. There were chairs too, and drugget on the floor, yet she told me that when she went to bed at night, and her father's voice came up from below reading the nightly chapter and praying to their terrible God that their children should be kept from sin — and he went into different kinds of sin to make all clear — for fear of His retribution, she felt so alone and afraid she dived down under the bedclothes, and yet could not go to sleep. I said stoutly that I didn't think God was like that, yet she felt who was I to know God better than such a family?

"The Room", of course, was not in general use. All I remember is that it was full of dark furniture, and that in it Mrs Saville kept her "machine". Her great treasure was an ancient sewing machine that Saville had bought in the market when Alice was born. She made all their clothes on it: all her men's shirts and nightshirts, everything she and the girls wore, turning old things into new clothes without the slightest fear. She had a store of patterns accumulated over the years, and fashion never came into it yet they always looked neat and nice. I suspect that quite a lot of garments came up from the Hall via the ladies' maid, and they certainly could not have been put to better use. And of course, everything was beautifully finished off by hand. Her buttonholes were exquisite. Nothing in that house was bought ready-made unless it were the "Measter's" best clothes. I know she made his working ones.

The kitchen I know so well, yet all I can see is the gleaming great range with the steel fender, and fire irons with great shining balls, and the steel topped guard round, where she aired sheets and shirts; then the table in the middle with its tapestry cloth, dulled with years of wear, and the wheezy old harmonium in the corner where Evaline painfully tried to play scales. Once when I played some hymn tunes, Mrs Saville to my astonishment produced from the depths of a cupboard a concertina — she rhymed it with Dinah — and joyfully squeezed out some chords. Now I know why poor Evaline endured those music lessons; she had no music in her at all but her mother had, and here was one thing in which she had not been able to fulfil herself but was trying to give to her daughter.

I don't suppose Saville's wage was more than a pound a week, and on the surface their life was Spartan, but behind the scenes they lived very well. As they said, "she" couldn't count the apples on the trees, nor the eggs laid, nor the hatchings out, nor even the piglets in all the litters, and there were many hidey-holes that even "her" sharp eyes could not discover, nor Train ferret out. I know we had a beautiful piece of boiled bacon for breakfast — very fat, but that was how they liked it up north — and I ate more meat that weekend than in a month normally. The apple pie melted in my mouth, and as for the cream, well, I had never tasted cream before, and to their great regret it made me feel sick and I had to refuse a second helping. It was explained to me that all this was for a treat because I was a guest, but I remember Evaline walked into it all as to the manner born, and showed no sign of surfeit.

The rooms were dark as the windows were very small — these houses were built to keep the outside out — and although it was May and the evenings were longish, it was too dark to see to sew and Mrs Saville took her work and a little hard chair out into her garden and sat till it was too dark to see at all. In the winter Mr Saville sat in his high-backed wooden armchair and read stumblingly by the light of a tallow dip as his wife sewed. Their few books were of the stern variety, and took him years to get through. He was on *Wuthering Heights* when I knew them. They were very parsimonious with light, I suppose because it was one of the things they had to pay real money for. They had a lamp but it was very rarely lighted. They always went to bed well before nine o' clock, for of course they both had to be up by dawn. They talked to each other very little, I think just to be together was enough, and I never saw the slightest demonstrativeness between them; nor did I ever see them kiss Evaline or she them, yet the love between them all could be felt directly you entered the house.

I was a silly fool and had never lived in a house with a man in it — to my recollection — and on the Sunday morning when Mr Saville was shaving in the back kitchen with a cut-throat razor, a weekly ritual, I rushed at him and threw my arms around his neck. At least, that's what I meant to do, but he nearly jumped out of his skin, and held me off with his left arm and shouted something at me. I felt and obviously looked so wretched that he explained patiently afterwards that I might have made him cut himself badly, but I think that even if he had not had the razor in his hand he would have been just as outraged.

Evaline and I had two lovely walks; one was to Askwith and down a footpath to the river where it was quite wide, and there was a busy mill, and the mill wheel working, and a great wide torrent of water falling over a stone dam. There were wide stepping-stones lower down where one could cross the river to the next village which was very hilly, clambering up and up. I had explored so much by myself, so I told Evaline I knew another way back, and I proved right. We only had to follow the path less than half a mile along our side of the water, wriggle through some wire, and we were against the bluebell slope, and there on the other side was the waterfall, and she had never seen any of them. We walked back along the river, past my boat, and round past the church and stables and back gate of the Hall, and up the wooded tunnel to the farm. We felt like real explorers, though Evaline was very timorous in any place she did not know.

We went next day to a field on the far side of the estate where I had never been, and had to skirt the cultivated fields to get to it, where, she said, her father said there had been a battle in one of the civil wars. It was a very flat field, and all round the four sides of it was a deep bank where the soldiers killed in the battle had been buried. Mr Saville had dug a little to test it, and there sure enough, were bones. It was a lush field, with buttercups and big ox-eye daisies, and on the slopes were the flat leaves of primroses that had finished blooming, and a scent of violets always seemed to linger after the flowers had gone, and I thought it a much lovelier resting place than that rank, mouldy little churchyard behind the stables at the Hall.

When Mother and Doff returned, Mother was in a dreadful temper. Something had obviously happened but I was not told what; I found later that Jessie was getting married and Doff had been to see her, and they had arranged that when I left school, Doff would go to Jessie's office to work with her and take her place when she left, providing she was good enough. To Mother this was rank treason on Doff's part, but it was Jessie, the viper, who was blamed. Doff had to bear a lot of "more in sorrow than in anger" stuff, as Mother hadn't known they were in touch with each other, but I think it was very good of Jessie to be bothered with any of us. It wasn't as if she had any affection for us or we had been close in any way. However, for me this last summer was a happy one. I had Miss Tinniswood, and we had a coronation and celebrations, a tea in the field at Askwith, and the following week a ride in a wagonette to Bradford to see a film of the coronation. I think we were too bewildered to take in much of it. The presentation was pretty bad, and we sat right in the front. The sudden jerkings and twitchings and flashings of the gigantic images on the screen, and the blare of the music that was played, together with sitting in the dark, which terrified us all, pretty well overlaid any enjoyment there might have been. Still, we knew God Save the King, and joined in singing that at the end. We were not used to crowds of course, and many of the smaller children were weepy by the time we got to our rather scruffy restaurant for tea. And when they were taken into the lavatories and heard the rushing water when the chains were pulled they screamed with terror and refused to "go". The finishing touch was when, slightly soothed with tea and buns, we emerged into the crowded street and two black men came along the pavement. Bedlam was let loose, and though we did eventually get back to our transport, and home, I shouldn't think any of those children would remember

126

that outing with any pleasure at all. I am sure the two teachers didn't.

The school summer holidays started at the end of July, I think, and at the end of my first week home Dorothy left us. Mother had a face like stone but did not say anything, and I started down at the laundry again. I wasn't fourteen till the end of September, but no-one said anything and life went on pretty much as it had before Doff had come. Mrs Dawson accepted me again but I don't think she was pleased for we did not last very long. Doff wrote to me occasionally — she did get Jessie's job — and had Dith come and work as her junior. She must have covered up for her a lot as Dith knew nothing of office work, but she started learning in London. However they lived I do not know for their pay was pitiful. Either Dith wasn't good enough, or did not like the job, as she left and went somewhere else, and Doff said I was to learn all I could and come to London when I was sixteen. However, I hadn't Doff's determination, and I could not, that first winter, go into Otley three times a week after work in the face of Mother's opposition. Besides, I had no money. Doff had wages, however small. I had none.

People were beginning to be quite nice to me. I had reached puberty and become, miraculously, nice looking and better dressed. We used occasionally to buy a copy of *Exchange and Mart*, and in the small ads people offered for sale their unwanted clothing very cheaply. We used to send for a "mixed parcel" of women's clothing, for perhaps half a crown — that was quite a lot to us — and I can remember some neat, pretty dresses that I altered and enjoyed wearing. I proved to be very good at taking in and turning up and letting down, and Mrs Saville encouraged me, though I know my stitching would not have passed Mrs White's critical standards.

Stockings and shoes were my worst difficulties, for one could not make them, and it was a long time before I ever had a really new pair of shoes. We would buy them through the paper, but other people's shoes never fit one as they should, and anyhow, a decent second-hand pair cost more than several dresses. New stockings cost 6 3/4d a pair, those black woollen ones with "Botany Wool" in red stitching round the top, but I wore them out so very quickly with my ill-fitting shoes, which I always had to wear long after they had holes in. I used to pad them with brown paper and water coming through isn't good for stockings. Apart from working all day, I was rather irresponsible that winter. I was not at all interested yet in boys — though plenty of other girls of fourteen were — but three of them were interested in me. They were all nice; just big boys who had outgrown their loutishness, and I enjoyed their friendship very much — though how I managed three at a time without any clashing I do not remember.

One was Frank Saville and he only came home one Sunday a month, but I would go over to the farm early to tea, and he and Evaline and I would roam around the whole place until it was dark, and then go and sit in the bakehouse by the fire and toast teacakes and eat plum bread — he could eat like a horse. Evaline would be running around after the kittens or some other young things, and Frank and I would talk and talk — or I did, he listened — and just then I thought I knew everything. I read every newspaper and magazine I got hold of and thought I was an ardent socialist and knew how to put the whole world to rights. I had practically decided to be a politician and one of the first women in Parliament when I had become educated — though how I was to become educated without any effort on my part I really don't know. The only trouble was I wanted to be a great singer, and I knew I could be a great writer. How people would have laughed had they known the dreams that went on in the head of one silly country girl. After tea I went to Chapel with them, and the usual order of walking was changed, for Frank and I walked behind Mr Saville.

Then there was Dick Blayes, a boy of sixteen who came over every Sunday morning with Harry Wigglesworth who played the church harmonium. They came on their bicycles and after the service Harry would say he had to hurry home, and Dick would push his bike, me walking with him round the back to the Hall gates half way to Otley, then say "Oh, I'll walk back home with you" and we would go along the Avenue through the Park and round the back way to Weston, and I expect he got into trouble with his mother for being late for dinner. Every week, regularly, he brought me the *Gem* and I wallowed in the doings of Dick Wharton and his friends.

The friend I saw most of was Charles Whitworth, who was "studying", of all things, gardening under Mr Clarkson the Head Gardener. I suppose that meant that he was working for very little more than his keep, and learning practical gardening on the spot. His father was a lecturer in horticulture in Leeds, and must have had ideas on the subject. Charles had been to a grammar school until he was sixteen, but I don't think he was particularly clever, although he did read and think as much as he could. He used to get books from the Mechanics Institute Library in Otley: Ruskin and Tolstoy and Marx, very heady stuff for a youngster like me if I could have understood half of it, but for light relief he always brought Sexton Blake and half a pound of Mackintosh's Toffees. Egg and Milk was my favourite; it was broken up in lumps in those days, and was much more succulent than the emasculated, twice-wrapped product we get now. So we sat every Saturday evening and ate and read and talked. Mother was there but she never minded. Mr Clarkson minded, though, for Charles was supposed to be intensely respectable and we were not, but though he apparently chided Charles for coming he never said anything to Mother or me, and then we left in the April, so all his worries were over.

Frank was a short, thickset serious boy, with his mother's dark hair and steady eyes. Dick was tall and fair with the merriest blue eyes imaginable, and Charles had curly red hair and red bristles, because he was so very spotty he couldn't shave as often as he ought. I thought of them a lot after 1914, pictured them gaily striding down the street at Otley with the other young men to join up, and felt pride in them. I had a shock when I had forwarded to me a letter from Charles, which said that with his views he could not believe in war and was a pacifist, and he knew I would agree with him, and he had never met a girl he could like as much as me and would I write to him. I did, once, and a very unkind letter it was. Bursting with patriotism as I was, and really grieved because I was a girl and could not go and fight for my country, to have Charles ask me to share his cock-eyed and, I thought, cowardly views, was too much, and I told him I certainly would not write again unless I heard from him that he had joined up. He wrote again, but I did not answer. The young can be so cruel. They were such nice boys, and not once when I knew them did one of them offer to touch me, nor say one word that could be taken amiss.

Some time after Christmas, when I was fourteen, there was great excitement. We were to have a "Servants' Ball". This was the first since we had been at Weston, but Evaline had told me about past ones, and I had something on the lines of Cinderella's Ball in mind, but it didn't turn out like that. Not at all. The Servants' Hall had been cleared except for long tables down the middle, and chairs round the walls. I don't think there was even any attempt at decoration. The women servants wore their dresses or skirts and blouses instead of their neat print or black dresses and white aprons, and didn't look nearly as nice, and the men's suits were more cumbersome than their livery. There were plates of thick bread and butter and mounds of buns and a huge tea urn which dispensed gallons of strong tea, but I honestly cannot remember anything more exciting. After tea there was dancing to music from, I think, a phonograph with a large horn. I could not dance, of course, and neither could many of the others, but I do remember the chauffeur and his wife, both very large, balcony people — and she had a tremendous goitre, poor thing — sailing in the most stately fashion round and round the room like a pair of galleons, scattering children right and left. Evaline and I sat and watched, she in the seventh heaven and I feeling dreadfully self-conscious, when to my horror Miss Phyllis came and asked me to dance with her. I got up, but said, "I can't dance", to which she replied "It doesn't matter, there aren't any steps" so we started gyrating, in silence at first, until she broke out with "Oh you are so pretty, Edith said you were." I had no reply. I had been trying to think up something clever to say, to show how unusual I was, but this cut the ground from under me. After more silence she said, "And Edith says you are ever so clever too. I'm not." (Edith was the nice lady's maid.) This finished me, and all I could blurt out was a stupid cliché of Mother's — "And a fat lot of good that'll do me", and dropped her hands and scooted back to Evaline who was sitting with her soul in her eyes, wishing she were me. When we were allowed to leave she heaved a deep sigh and said that it wasn't like it used to be.

While I was still at school, Phyllis Dixon and I used to walk into Otley to do our weekly shopping every Saturday morning. She told me with refreshing candour that she came so as to get out of doing jobs at home. She was about my age, the second eldest girl, and rather wild and cheeky, but as I was looked upon as being wild as well, I suppose we made a pair. She pretended to keep up with my imaginative flights, and we called each other by boys' names, I forget what they were, and went on each weekend from episode to impossible episode, and I realised afterwards she always thought I was a bit daft. However, about the time I left school, they went to live in a new cottage in Askwith so my friendship with her ended, though occasionally when at a loose end, I would walk over there and kind Mrs Dixon always asked me to tea. She told me later that Phyllis was a sore worry to her. "You know, Gertie," she said, "I used to think you two were alike, but you are as different as can be. She takes after her father." She certainly did. I met her once or twice in the village, only my age, with some great lout's arm round her, giggling down the road, or rolling on the grassy bank by the stream. I turned my head and she would call out "Coo, aren't we a grand lady."

Once when I visited Mrs Dixon, her husband was there. Normally he stayed in the "Room" but I suppose he heard a strange female voice and came into the kitchen; I saw his nasty squinting eyes light up and he started talking to me in a soft soapy sort of voice. Hitherto he had never deigned to look at me, let alone speak. He looked me slowly up and down, and my flesh seemed to crawl. "Well, well, Gertie, we are growing up aren't we," he said, and he insisted on having tea in the kitchen with us, and talked to me in little soft whispers and made me feel horrible. "You sing, don' you, Gertie?" he said. "With your looks now and what your figure's going to be you should go on the stage." And he said he could give me an introduction to someone he knew, whenever I liked. I got away into the scullery with Mrs Dixon to help wash up as soon as I could, and she said "God forgive me for saying it of my husband, but he's a bad man. Don't have anything to do with him, but run off home now," and I did, and I didn't see him again.

CHAPTER
ELEVEN

The Dawsons always went away in early spring, and it was when they returned in April 1912 that we were given a week's notice to leave. No reason had to be given of course, but it was pretty awful to have literally to pick up our bed and walk at such short notice, for naturally we had not a penny by us. Our bed was not worth picking up, as it happened, and all else we had was a couple of small chairs, a kitchen table, the Hamper and a few pieces of crockery and kitchenware. And two cats. And here I committed my first crime, which I shall never forget. We had given to us, early in our time there, a sweet little fluffy kitten which was now a sweet little fluffy cat. In Askwith, on my wanderings, I was always seeing a pitiful, dirty, half bald white cat, which came to know me and would run to me when I passed. It belonged to the carrier, a man who was drunk half the time, and on one occasion as I passed, he was near his gate and caught the cat with a hefty kick. I said "Beast" but went on my way, but the next day, which was one of his journey days, I went back to his house with a rush basket and a skewer, popped the animal into the basket, closed the top with the skewer, and took it home. It seemed to have no energy and just lay still. From that day on, though, it was a different cat. It fought our Fluffy, ate the lion's share of the food and spent most of the day asleep on our bed. And then, horror of horrors, our little Fluffy began to go bald, and at the time of our getting notice, we had two half bald cats, one large, white and well-fed, and the other a little shivering semi-Persian, terrified of everything. Something had to be done about them. Mother said we would leave them behind, but I could not do that. I tried to give them away, but people just laughed and Mrs Saville would not have them at the farm, though I pointed out that two more among so many would not make any difference, but she said, with the sureness of experience, "How long will there be only two?" She also pointed out that Mrs Dawson would soon notice if all of the cats started going bald, because Miss Phyllis was "a rare one for the kittens".

So it came to the same old thing. If something had to be done I must do it myself. I procured a sack and a brick, put the two trusting animals in the former with the latter, stood on the neck of it while I tied it as firmly as I could with strong twine pinched from the barn, and in the semi-darkness staggered along with my squirming bundle to the pond. There I summoned up enough strength to swing it up so that it carried well away from the edge. The pond I chose was on the Manor land and was supposed to be unusually deep. Perhaps those poor animals haunted my sleep that night; I don't know, but they have haunted me many nights and days since during the last sixty-odd years.

There were a few high spots in my life at Weston, the traditional church holy days giving the excuse for some mild junketing, though in passing I must say I have never in my life known a community less conscious of religion, organised or otherwise. Easter was the first one of course, and as far as our lives were concerned, the only eggs we knew were laid by the backyard hens. In Otley market, however, we could buy some for a halfpenny each. These we would boil, and then either paint them, or wrap them in brightly coloured material and boil them again, after which, if we were lucky, they would emerge looking very gay indeed. I remember one batch that Evaline and I wrapped in pieces of old purple and yellow silk that we found caught on a hedge near Dawson's rubbish dump, and they looked really marvellous. These one distributed to one's friends and relations. On Easter Sunday all the young people made their way to Tom Moss's ghyll, a pretty, very hilly cutting off the bottom of Askwith village. Some families had quite a basket of eggs, and some, like me, might have up to half a dozen, and the object of the exercise was to roll an egg bumpitty from the top of the hill, and then tear down to catch it before it rolled into the rough little stream at the foot of the ghyll. If you pitched it off too hard it was soon in pieces, and if not hard enough it sat at the first ledge and you had to toil all the way up again, rescue it and start afresh. The right way to do it was in pairs or teams, and then the egg which got furthest without actually landing in the stream or breaking was the winner. The one that stuck en route went to the winner's owner. I rather think

137

the rules were elastic, according to the forcefulness of the players, but generally a good time was had by all, particularly when it was a really fine day, and a few nice mothers or elder sisters would turn up with baskets of bread and butter and enamel cans of tea. Then we would strip the shells off our eggs and eat them with the greatest enjoyment.

Whitsun was the next festival, or as they called it in Otley for obvious reasons White Sunday. The town children assembled by the church, the girls all wearing white dresses and the boys in large white collars, and most of them had brought white flowers. They then processed all around the town, the clergy and choirboys in their white surplices leading and the girls with their white flowers made up into garlands and with wreaths on their heads, following, and the other boys coming along behind. All around the central streets they went, through the Market Place and back to the church, and through the big main door like so many brides and grooms. I suppose they had a service or something but we were only onlookers and not invited, but trudged the three or four miles back to our village pulling branches of May off the hedges as we went.

Then there was a long stretch of time to the next event, which was Mischief Night, the 31st October, but we were preparing for this for quite a while. The most important thing was to practise making a good turnip lantern, and Mr Saville's stack of swedes was sadly depleted. We sat in the big barn and hacked and scraped until we had each produced something that satisfied us — not easy. One had to slice off all ugly

138

protuberances, cut off a slice for the lid, hollow out the inside leaving a thin enough shell for the light of a candle to shine through yet not so thin as to sag and break, and leave a ring at the bottom into which a candle would fit. One had to cut into the outer skin a pattern of stars and moon, or a witch's head or anything else fanciful, so that it showed up when the candle was lighted; then hollow out the lid, making four holes in it and in the main lantern, thread string through the holes, and hey presto there's your lantern! On the night we dressed up in outlandish clothes — not difficult for me — and blacked our faces with soot, of which we had plenty, and knocked at the door of each of the eight cottages and two farms — not of course at the Manor, the Grange or the Hall. There was a tag we were supposed to say, something about Mischief Men come knocking at your door, feed us if you've plenty but a crust if you are poor, but as we were gathered in at each cottage the moment we had knocked, I never had a chance of hearing it through. I have said the village people were inhospitable to strangers, but the inhospitality did not extend to the village bairns. Though they were sitting waiting for our knock they welcomed us like prodigal sons, and plied us with parkin, butterscotch and weak, home-made ginger wine, the same at each house. We must have been nearly bursting when the orgy was finished.

Next of course the Fifth of November, Bonfire Night. The men would have been carting wood up to the green, round which the new cottages were built, for a week, and a really noble bonfire was erected. All the

139

men turned out — it was about the only bit of fun they had — and I thought the display of fireworks they let off was wonderful, though they were nothing like the ones children have now. We roasted potatoes in the embers, and the women sent out more parkin, though they never came out themselves, only stood in their doorways to keep their eyes on the children; they were terribly nervous of them getting hurt. These were two wonderful days.

CHAPTER
TWELVE

Then came Christmas. Curiously enough, though Mother had tried to keep Christmas Day when we were two or three years younger, and all together, at Weston, it was no different from any other day, except that we did not go down to the laundry. Any Christmas the cottage people kept was inside their own houses with the doors shut and the curtains closed. We did not have decorations either, though I seem to remember cutting up paper and making chains at school. The fun and excitement of Christmas was going out carol-singing. A man who lived in the Grange cottages made a big thing of organising this, and did it very well considering the complete lack of talent available. He himself could wheeze a hymn tune out of the harmonium — he was Evaline's music teacher — and also scrape a very doubtful tune out of a fiddle, and had a large, harsh, off-key singing voice, but he loved music.

There were about a dozen children altogether and we sat around the pump with him a couple of weekends before Christmas and practised the best-known carols, though few knew the words. When he found I could tinkle on my mandolin he was enchanted, so I had to fetch it and we played a sort of accompaniment by ear

141

which sounded dreadful, but he said it was "champion". On the evening of the 23rd, in pitch darkness because our lantern wouldn't burn, we huddled outside the cottages and sang our carols. Several of the younger children were rather tearful because of the darkness and cold, but as soon as we started open came the doors, and the families were on the steps, and you'd have thought we were prima donnas, the praise they lavished on us. "Ee, Gertie, and yev brought yer banjo, and yer all singin beautiful." We sang our three carols and then had a hot mince pie and a slice of Yule bread, and then onto the next group of cottages where they were waiting behind the door, having heard all of our first performances. So we went through it again, to equal praise and rewards, and at the last group, knowing we were going on to the two farms, someone produced a lantern which worked, and the man carried it and I felt we were really quite professional.

As we passed the cottages again doors opened and small ones were plucked up — "Coom on, our Jackie, time thee were in thee bed," and we went on, depleted in number but not in quality. Over to Saville's, where the lantern, held aloft, sent a splash of bright light ahead and the shadows of our legs and bodies danced a weird fandango. Here we were taken inside the back kitchen and sang our carols and ate our mince pies and Yule bread, and drank ginger wine as a bonus, and very warming it was, then on to our last call at the Grange Home Farm.

142

I never liked going into the Grange farmhouse. It was the opposite of the Hall Farm in that it was dirty and had a miserable, unhappy atmosphere, a slatternly farm wife who never stopped talking, and a morose farmer whose every second word was an oath. They had had many babies, all but two of which had died, Alan the eldest boy, handsome but sullen like his father — he worked with him on the farm — and Evie, a pale, cheeky, whimpering, lying little brat who was the apple of her parents' eyes. Evie had to stand in the front of our little group, only about five or six now, and as far as her family was concerned, she sang the carols — she had a squeak like a mouse — and we merely accompanied her. However, we had our food, though where we put it I don't know, and managed to get away in spite of Mrs Holmes' unceasing eulogies on her daughter's cleverness in knowing all those words, and down the path her valediction floated. "Ee, faither, did yiver ear soocha loovly voice? Y'mun coom t' bed nah, ma loovey, else y'll be wore oot int'morning," and she hadn't even been out with us! Evie and Mr Holmes joined together in a quite unrepeatable injunction regarding getting out and shutting t' gate. But Christmas Eve was the wonderful night for me, for we went up on the moor to several shepherds' cottages and small farmhouses. Not children this time, but about a dozen men of all ages and me, with the fiddler's daughter to keep me company. Until I was turned fourteen my voice was full and sweet and quite strong, and I sang a solo verse in each carol, and gave myself a rest in the others. How I loved it!

Another fiddle had turned up from somewhere, and each man had a lantern on a stick, and we stood in our pool of light, singing to just one family clustered in their lighted doorway, with perhaps no-one else for half a mile but miles of moorland stretching away all round us, and no other sound but the occasional sheep's cough, or a night bird hunting.

After our carols we went into the cottage and were regaled with Christmas fare and the men with home-made wine. At first they were careful, saying we had a long way to go and needed steady hands and feet, but for the last half of our round many of the heads were getting muddled. I think I was nearly asleep on my feet when a trap appeared with a horse in the shafts, and Edna and I were bundled in a blanket and hoisted in the back, and a kindly farmer drove us to our homes. I think the men carried on until all the folk on Askwith Moor had heard the Christmas message — not more than a dozen dwellings, perhaps, but more than a dozen miles before the weary-footed men reached their homes, and that after a day spent working in the fields or at the forge.

CHAPTER
THIRTEEN

We went to a tiny terraced house in Otley of the wicked old "back to back" variety, but it was a mill town and two-thirds of the ordinary residents lived in the same way, so we were quite respectable. This was beginning to mean quite a lot to me. Mother decided to take in washing until we found another job, and bought a stove and some irons, and possibly a tub or two on HP and we trailed round from door to door asking for patronage. We did know quite a few tradespeople in the town, and one or two recommended us, but it wasn't enough to keep us going. Miraculously, the most respectable draper's shop offered to take me as a learner at half a crown a week, and my dinner and tea. This put me right up in the social scale but one of the two women who owned the shop was very religious and a cat to work for. I found that Dick Blanes was apprenticed to a barber in the same row of shops, and though he popped out whenever he saw me pass, we had precious little time to renew our friendship, besides which his mother would know about it in Otley. I did somehow get to know a few young girls, but my little spare time was spent either trying to get more work, helping with what little there was, or delivering. One man in Otley was a great friend to us. He had been our insurance agent, and used to come out to Weston one evening a month to collect our two-penny premium. He was in charge of the little office in the town and took us to his home to meet his young wife and baby, so it gave us a bit of a background, and he got us some work. But Mother could not possibly do laundry under such conditions. We hadn't anywhere clean and airy to hang clothes and spent ages trying to clean black smuts off the finished articles, and very soon we lost what trade we had and Mother would be waiting outside the draper's shop for my miserable half crown. We had to leave the terraced house and moved into a horrible back alley; I think the houses were derelict and we just gate-crashed and paid no rent. They were filthy and the windows were broken and everything was covered with a coating of black grit.

In the one next to us there was what would now be called a problem family. I don't know what was wrong with the parents. There were about twelve children, the youngest ones rolling about the filthy floor naked. The place wasn't furnished, only rags and boxes, but the older girls were delicate and charming-looking. Their mother just sat looking pleasant and suckling the latest baby, in dirty rags, and a harmless looking man went in and out, and spoke to us quite politely. I remember seeing vague shapes at some of the other houses.

I had seen a tall young man stalking me almost since we came to Otley. At first it was him and his friend but later it was him alone. I got used to seeing him, but managed to avoid direct contact. I didn't know him and was becoming ashamed of our position. It was curious in that society, there were such layers and they didn't mix. There were apparently definite rules; the young of opposite sexes did not mix. If a young man sought a girl's company and spoke to her, and she allowed it, then they were "keeping company" and as such, respectable, but casual meeting was frowned upon. So unknowingly I did the right thing in avoiding him. He found we had left our house, and could not find out where we had moved to. He started waiting outside the shop for me to come out, and I was so ashamed of the conditions under which we were living that I managed to give him the slip by doubling back on my tracks. But one night he cheated, hurried, came round in front of me and said "Good evening". As I didn't answer he said what he had apparently rehearsed, "I am John Thwaite, Improver, through my apprenticeship. Can I walk home with you?" I had nothing to say, so he fell in step with me and told me he had been trying for weeks to meet me, as if I didn't know, and said his father was a master man and his mother would "receive" me. He looked very manly and straightforward, but all I wanted was to get away before he saw the horrible hole I was going to. But there was no help for it, and I turned into that awful alley before he realised I was going to. He stopped, gave one look at the rotting place, and one at me, and I saw his eyes widen with horror and disgust. "So this is where you hide yourself," he said and turned and almost ran away. He meant nothing to me but I felt sick with humiliation.

Generally speaking, the local girls were not pretty. They were squat and dark, and hard-looking. I suppose it was years of working in the mills from early childhood, and the local water made their teeth very bad. Their envy of my height and colouring and, yes, my looks, was under my circumstances, very reassuring, and one of them told me about a most eligible young man who had been making enquiries about me, and told me how lucky I was. I quite pertly said I wasn't interested.

A day or two later Mother heard from a "Hydro" in Ben Rhydding whose advertisement she had answered, and we were just about on our beam ends when a letter came giving us the job, so we left our miserable bed behind us — and I am afraid a lot of debts too — and moved ourselves. Ben Rhydding was not many miles away, a tiny high-class moorland village, and the Hydro, whatever that was, was well away from the village, high up on the rolling moors. Up behind it were great famous rocks much bigger than houses, and rushing streams and waterfalls. I had no idea what the name meant, and thought it was something to do with magic, for I had read about the Hydra-headed monster that turned people to stone, and as there were iron-stone springs all over the moors I thought it was something to do with petrifying people. After all, there was Mother Shipton's Well.

It turned out to be a large hotel where rich folk went for holidays, and to drink the waters of the spring that welled up in the grounds and were piped into what had been a white marble bath-cum-fountain, but was now stained brownish-red from the iron deposits. There were two other women working under Mother, and the four of us did the work for the guests in the hotel and all the staff, and as it was "the season" very hard work it was. I remember very little about the laundry except that we worked a full twelve hour day, that I had to pull my weight with the others, and that I formed the habit of fainting frequently.

It was around this time that I found to my sorrow that my full singing voice left me, and I was left with a sweet little warble that tightened up and hurt in my middle if I tried to sing louder. The other two laundresses were friends who took jobs together. One was fair and rather pretty, a yielding and soft kind of person, while the other was a dark, waspish virago, very possessive where her friend was concerned. They both sang very well — perhaps it's the steam in a laundry that makes a laundress's voice clear and good, I wouldn't know, but they sang beautifully the whole time as they worked, unless the dark one was in an ill humour, when she nagged. They were certainly never quiet. The dark one and Mother quarrelled from the start, they were too much alike. I shared quite a nice bedroom with Mother on the attic floor, and the other two were next door. We had our meals in a big servants' dining hall, and the food was good and plentiful, and I expect, helped to keep me going. I was very happy at the weekends, roaming for miles on the moors, and in the other direction, through the village back to my old river, where the mill and the stepping stones were, but I did not like the dining hall and the other servants.

There was an atmosphere which I dimly knew was a mixture of greed and sex.

The hotel servants had artificially genteel voices when working, but when they were round the table together they were coarse and foul. They told dirty stories, the men especially, and bragged about their affairs with the women guests, and nudged and leered and winked, and the female servants encouraged them. Occasionally the cook would say, with a warning glance at me sitting quiet, "Little pigs have long ears," but they didn't really care. It was as well the guests did not know what these apparently courteous, almost servile people said about them behind their backs. They sneered about people's night attire and clothes and the dressing table things they had brought with them, and the size of their tips.

The men were all married; they took these jobs for the season, leaving their wives at home, and they would talk unpleasantly about them and about marriage in general. They were rather a cosmopolitan mixture, and though you would not have thought it from their appearance, must have been the lowest of the low. They worked in shifts of course, and when their mates were absent spoke just as horribly about them, though to their faces they were the best of friends. I got so that the talk flowed over me and escaped directly meals were over, but for a long time I felt dirty when I thought about these people. I thought the men hanging round the pretty laundress were like the village dogs after Mr Saville's sheepdog when she was on heat.

There wasn't a servants' sitting room, and we used to go to our bedroom after the evening meal, and quite soon to bed. Sometime while we were in Weston Mother had given me a mandolin — I had wanted a violin — and I had learned to tinkle any tune on it, and I would sit up in bed while Mother read, and play and play and croon to it, and I have often wondered since what guests on the floor below thought about the noise, for I was very strict with myself and would practise tremolo for ages.

One incident stands out in my memory of this place. There was to be a ball given by the Manageress for her young sister, who was eighteen and at a ballet school. There was to be an orchestra, and fancy dress, and all the guests would be invited; the staff talked about it for some time beforehand, with many ill-natured comments. On the night of the ball, the housekeeper, whom I had seldom seen and who was a very different type from the other servants, asked me if I would like to watch. Of course I said, "Yes, please," and she took me to a big empty upstairs room at one end of which was a glass partition, a part of which she slid back. She put a chair to one side of the open space and told me I could stay there as long as I liked so long as I stayed silent and out of sight. Below me was what seemed a tremendous room, beautifully decorated with flowers with coloured lights intertwined, as well as glass chandeliers. The music started, I could not see the players, and gradually the room filled up with people in every conceivable costume, many very beautiful and some grotesque, and they seemed so happy, so

151

animated, I could be happy with them. And then there was a lull. The door opened, the crowd parted, the music started again and there entered the most beautiful thing I had ever seen. The Queen of the Night like the one in my picture book, a girl, about as tall as me, standing under the bright lights, every detail clear. Her face was pale and her dark hair hung like a black cloak, glittering like the Milky Way and in front was one shining star on her forehead. Her dress was black, her bodice clung to her and her skirts were a cloud of long, diaphanous draperies, dotted with little twinkling stars of different sizes.

She stood still, making a lovely entrance, and then sank into a deep curtsy. Everyone clapped and then shouted applause. She rose up flushing a tiny bit, and looking so happy and so sure of all the admiration round her, and something came up inside me through to my chest, and something else right up to my head. I thought I would faint with the immensity of my feeling, but instead tears welled up — the only time I really remember — and I sat there for all of two hours with my head in my hands and sobbed my heart out. I think it was a mixture of beauty overwhelming my senses, and envy at the realisation of the chasm dividing this girl from me. Self-pity is a soul-destroying thing, as I early realised, and, thank God, had the sense to fight against, but that night was one of the worst times I have had in my life.

The intensity of feeling when one is young is so much stronger than people allow for, and for a week after I was a pale washed-out thing, like a sawdust doll

152

with the stuffing nearly gone. I could not tear myself away, even when I recovered somewhat, the colours and the music called me too much.

At the end of September the season was over and we were given our marching orders, they could manage with the other two women; but Mother did have rather more notice this time and we were able to go straight to another job, in Derbyshire in a country house in hunting country. We had a little flat this time in the same building as the laundry, with a sitting room, neat kitchen and bedroom with two beds, each with an eiderdown. The laundry quarters were part of one side of a square courtyard, the other sides being the stables and the head groom's house. The stables had half doors of course, and it was lovely to see those shining heads and necks. There was always something to watch from our windows, either the men grooming them, or leading them out to exercise or bringing them back, or the family visiting them or bringing friends round to see them and having them brought out and trying their paces. The red-letter day was when the hunt would meet; the hounds would mill about and it was all very busy and exciting. The big gates leading to the lawns of the house would be opened. The gentry would ride into the courtyard with their grooms leading spare horses and the women would sit beautifully, looking so proud and aloof, till some gentleman to whom they were talking put out his hand, and they put their foot in it and slid down gracefully, and after inspecting the horses in the loose boxes wandered through the gates to have drinks on the lawn.

The lady and gentleman of the house were an American heiress and her husband who had married her — according to the servants — for her money. I thought her very beautiful and he was like Prince Charming. But the servants were unpleasant and speculated on how long the marriage would last, and when she would start a baby, and grumbled at how tightly she held the purse strings. I got to know the head gardener and his wife and young family, but the house servants and the four grooms seemed very grown up and remote.

At Christmas the family went away; early on the morning of Christmas Day I heard singing outside. I got up and looked out and there was a young maid with two grooms singing "Christians Awake!" to us. I was thrilled and excited, perhaps this day would turn out to be a bit different. I got dressed in a hurry and went down and opened the door and they came in with, of all things, a bottle of whisky. Of course we didn't have anything for them, but they came back later with an invitation from the cook for us to go to dinner. This was wonderful. I was nearly delirious with happiness, for they were making such a lot of me, it seemed as if they really cared, and I had been feeling pretty friendless. Mother just took it all passively, and said nothing against any of it. We had a lovely dinner, after which everyone just sat and drank, until even ignorant I had to realise they were all drunk. No-one was offensive or noisy, just stupid, women and men, and when I kept pushing away the arm of the young groom next to me

154

he didn't mind, merely slid it back a few minutes later until he finally subsided with his head on my knee.

The cook sat back in her corner. Someone called for some songs, and a man who was pushed to his feet sang a lot of what were probably local folk songs. They weren't music hall songs — but they became more and more suggestive, and I blushed inwardly and thought I must be misunderstanding him. Then even he slipped down in his chair and fell asleep, but the cook didn't, and eventually I slid out from under the groom and Mother and I got up and went back to our laundry and nobody noticed. However, all was back to normal next day, and when the family came back, Mother was told that we were "not suitable", and would have to go. I always felt that the other servants took against us, but I could not understand why, nor why they should want us to lose our place. Once again Mother had time to write around for another one, and got a good situation at an orphanage in Hull, but it was for her only, living in, so we went back to Otley and it was arranged that I should stay with Mrs Stopes until Mother found somewhere for me in Hull. (Mr Stopes had been the insurance agent who was friendly to us.) He was so kind to us, and charged Mother so little for my board that his wife was not pleased and did not cease to rub it in to me.

Their little house was one of a long terrace, all down one side of a street, with identical ones on the other side. They were comparatively new, with a big room and a little kitchen downstairs, a big bedroom and a tiny one upstairs, and they lived in the kitchen and small bedroom. The big rooms were kept polished and dusted with all the best hideous furniture and ornaments for the visitors who never came, except me. She hated me sleeping in her lovely brass bedstead. Even in these newish houses the front door was right on the pavement, and there was the tiniest piece of ground at the back mostly occupied by the privy and mangle. The back door was always open and she gossiped interminably with her next-door neighbour. They lived their lives at these back doors when they weren't polishing or scrubbing, and everything said was related to their poor husbands when they came home from work.

I expect they had very little money, and they didn't eat much, or at least she didn't, but I had a good appetite and I was very hungry while I was with them. In the evenings I would sit and think about food, about our Christmas dinner, about pieces of bread and thick butter, and lumps of cheese. Our evening meal always consisted of a small bowl of synthetic soup, made from a square of compressed powder boiled in water (one square to the three of us and the lion's share to the man) and one piece of bread. I would wash up in the little sink in the corner and scrabble about looking on the shelves for a stray piece of biscuit or anything else that might have been overlooked, then go to bed ravenously hungry and couldn't sleep. Then after two weeks when I was desperate Mother wrote saying I was to come.

I went by train to Hull and remember nothing of the journey except that I felt desperately ill. I had in fact fainted when I got up, and Mrs Stopes and I kept it from Mr Stopes in case he should say I must not go. I know I had only my straw case to carry, but when I changed somewhere a young porter, seeing my pale face I suppose, went to take it from me; but I said "No, no," because I couldn't afford to tip him, but he just took it and trotted me along to a carriage and settled me comfortably, to my great relief. Mother had arranged for me to stay at the Girls' Friendly Society Boarding House, and had made me a member directly she reached Hull for this express purpose. The idea of the homes when they were started was to do just this; to house young women living away from home — or who had no home — at a cheap rate, and to take in just a few higher paying ordinary boarders to help cover costs. Economic pressure, I suppose, had made it function the other way round. It was a boarding house of moderate price for genteel ladies, which took a G.F.S. member for a night or two if really necessary. They did not bargain for girls like me and I was quite a shock.

CHAPTER
FOURTEEN

The house was not far from the railway station and I had been told how to get there, and when, in response to my timid ring on the doorbell, the maid opened the door, she looked at me as if I were something the cat had left on the step. Miss Smith the housekeeper came fussing along, sent the maid away, tut-tutted at me in displeasure because I looked so pale, and took me up two long flights of stairs to my room. She was a tall, well-proportioned lady with short-sighted eyes, and pince-nez on a button on her dress with a long cord. She wore ropes of beads which jangled as she walked and on the other side of the button, a watch pinned with a brooch. Her hair was in a bun on top of her head and she was fitted with large false teeth which snapped at me but smiled at other guests. She explained in basic English that the boarding house did not exist for girls like me, that I should keep myself out of the way of the ladies, and that at mealtimes I should speak when spoken to. She also hoped my mother would soon remove me. In the meantime I could unpack my things, supper was at seven and I could stay in my room till then. I also learned that the two Misses Yates who lived there were sisters to the curate at St Mark's, and daughters of a Rector. Miss Lindsay was a Froebel schoolteacher, in a large fee-paying school in the town, also a daughter of the Church, and engaged to a doctor.

I was too tired by now to feel really hungry, but had a good hot wash in the bathroom — the first bathroom since institution days, and a great joy to me — made myself as neat as I could and lay down on the bed to wait for the gong. Then I crept downstairs with my heart somewhere just below my throat, and lacked the courage to go through the door marked "Dining Room". So I was chid for being late. But once I started, how I did enjoy my meal. As far as food was concerned I was treated the same as the others.

The Misses Yates were elderly spinsters, one short, one tall; both were grey haired, both plain, both thought themselves still youngish and interesting. They had a great interest in, and admiration of, "gentlemen". Their father had been one, their brother was one, and the fact that these "gentlemen" had seen fit to let them grow up without training of any kind, and left them to exist on a very small income till they grew old and died, never entered their heads. They still bridled and preened if anything male came near them — anything in their station of life, that is. They had a great knowledge of "stations", and had they deigned could have told you the order of precedence of all the rectors and vicars and canons and deans and bishops, yes and the Royal Family too. The tall one, the younger, was well under her sister's thumb, and constantly being reminded of her junior position.

They referred to "our dear mother" and "our respected father" and quoted their precepts endlessly. In fact, except for their lack of kindliness, they were very like a pair out of *Cranford*. They hardly ever spoke to me, but talked "at" me quite a bit, and I felt sorry for Miss Smith who was terrified of them. I thought them a pair of old cats, but Miss Lindsay said they were old fussies. Miss Lindsay was beautiful in looks and nature, with a fine-trained mind and a lovely sense of fun as well as a sense of humour, not always the same thing. She came from the same background as the Misses Yates, but had no sense of her own importance, just a natural grave dignity when necessary. She certainly knew how genteel people had to work to keep up appearances on next to nothing; she had obviously felt it keenly all her life. She had a sister married to a clergyman and was devoted to her, and appeared to spend quite a lot of her salary on her young nephews and nieces. When the Misses Yates in the most ladylike way questioned her on why she kept her young doctor waiting, she would say wryly that some people had to wait until they could afford to marry and have a family. Of course, this was wrong. You did not mention children until they happened or God sent them, or whatever it was.

I adored Miss Lindsay from afar, but though we never had any real conversation she would send many a one-sided smile or twinkle along in my direction when the Misses Yates were riding their hobby horses. These ladies spent their days attending the multitudinous services in their brother's church, which was very "high" — there were about half a dozen a day, I think. He used to wear a stole, whatever that was, and they used incense and there was a great deal of chanting, and they used to retail it all to Miss Smith at meal times. She was a member of this congregation too, but could not attend as often as they did, so had to drag herself out to early Mass. One day Mr Yates came to tea. They didn't hang flags out, but they did everything else they could to celebrate. Their tea was served in Miss Smith's sitting room. I saw him in the hall, and a very small rabbitty man he looked, with a huge Adam's apple over his dog collar. Their great worry was that some designing female of his congregation should lure him into marriage, but I don't think they had much to worry about.

Mother had a job lined up for me and I had to go and see about it the day after I arrived, ready to start the following Monday. It was not in a laundry, but in the receiving office of a laundry, and in a bad part of the city, a back street off the Hessle Road. The owner was a large, fat, fair man who should have been placid, but looked unhappy and harassed; his elder daughter was about twenty and very like him, and obviously they were good friends. She spoke bossily to me, and I found I was to be in this office with the younger daughter, to do the work of sorting out and labelling the stuff that came in, and wrapping it up and handing it out again and being responsible for the money. Also, apparently, I was to be responsible for the daughter, for, her father said gloomily, "she is like her Mother, a bitch". The office was open from nine to seven on weekdays, and till ten on Saturdays. I lasted two weeks, not because I couldn't cope with the place but with the daughter. When I met her I thought she was great fun, about my own age and a bit outrageous, for she said the most awful things about her father and sister. I found that her mother was Italian, had run away with some man after several previous affairs, and would probably soon come home after this one. My charge, Bianca, was very dark and pretty and quite man-mad; most of the young men in that far from tame neighbourhood were after her. Her sister's name was Gladys!

I had to rush to get there in the morning because breakfast was at eight, and I had to walk, having no money for a bus fare, and Miss Smith nearly threw a fit when I arrived home at twenty to eleven on Saturday, because doors were locked at ten. Bianca had been quite well-behaved, only teasing me and sending sidelong looks at a group of youths who would hang around outside and inside the shop, but did not argue when I said they must stay outside. However, things had been better arranged by the following Saturday, for well before closing time half a dozen of them were in the shop and would not leave, and she sat on our side of the counter and smiled and made silly, provocative remarks and then they were fighting in and out of the shop and Bianca thought it was heaven. A windowpane was broken and the police came and there was an awful to-do. Her father was sent for and he said I was no use and I finally got back to the boarding house just before midnight. I did not go back and Mother had to support me until I found something else.

In the free day or two I had, before starting at the laundry, I had arranged to attend Evening Institute classes in commercial subjects. I don't remember signing on or whether the classes were free or not, but I know Mother had to pay for the books which must have been a blow for her. The classes were on three nights a week and covered shorthand, typing, commercial geography, English, French and book-keeping and were held at the Girls' Grammar School. It was difficult, while I was at the receiving office, to get there on time, and I only did it by missing my evening meal, and with Bianca's help, though she did not understand why anyone would want to go to school. The atmosphere of that school building did something to me, and though I had a terrible inferiority complex, inside myself I gloried in being there and felt myself to be part of the place. I tortured myself a lot by thinking if I had behaved differently to Mrs Brown at Askwith I might have gone to an even better school, but I knew really Mother had vetoed it anyhow. I did well; it really seemed at that time as if I couldn't learn too much, though in the actual technical business of typing many others were better than I was. The English mistress positively crooned over me. Oddly enough, we studied Ruskin's *Sesame and Lilies* that first term, and I had read it with Charles, though I didn't understand it. No-one knew what an ignorant uneducated girl I was, or anything about my background, and as I was still wearing shoes and things we had been able to buy while at Ben Rhydding or Littleover, I wasn't too badly dressed. As I sneaked into the bathroom whenever I could I wasn't "antisocial", so I was accepted and absorbed.

It was during this first term that I met the four boys with whom I was friendly all the time I was in Hull: Billy and his friends Frank, Dick and Steve. Every school evening we gravitated together, just kids. One night Billy pointed through a glass door to where a girl with a great thick rope of flaxen hair was doing something with one or two other day school girls and said "Look, that's Jess, she's the School Captain and she's a sort of cousin of mine. Our parents have a kind of arrangement about us, for when we're older". I felt green with envy, because she did look nice, somehow, but I didn't say anything.

I tramped the streets every day and went to the Labour Exchange where the kind woman at the desk found me a problem. I didn't fit neatly into her categories. I didn't look strong enough for one kind of job, was too young for another, but she did send me to some kind of factory where they wanted young girls. I have always been grateful to the woman in charge there for her kindness. She was most annoyed with the Labour Exchange people for sending me, and said to me, "This work is not for you, and you must never mix with the type we have here. They would kill your soul in a month. Whatever happens, no matter how long it takes, promise you will only try to get office work." So, feeling pretty hopeless, for I knew how Mother needed me to earn money, I promised, and as no office jobs offered for a bit, I had a blissful week or two exploring Hull. I wasn't interested in ordinary shops. People talk

164

about the pleasures of window-shopping, but there is none when you have no money in your pocket, and no possibility of having any. All you get from looking at beautiful things you would like to wear is longing and envy, and that does no-one any good, but what I did love were the old shops in the narrow twisting streets towards the sea. At first they were very high class, full of lovely old things from all over the world, and shipping company offices with pictures of many places. As they went nearer the sea there were "ships' chandlers" and shops that smelled of tarred rope, and with all sorts of things I did not know the use of, dark dusty shuttered places with upper storeys leaning over, and ropes and pulleys and things.

I stayed in this seaport side of Hull, not the Old Town; that, of course, was a part where ordinary people dared not go. Even policemen had to walk in twos. Down Blackfriargate and the long new road to what looked like the sea, but was really of course the River Humber, there was a long pier. Here one could sit and watch the comings and goings of innumerable small boats and some biggish ones too, and look across to Immingham dimly seen in the distance, and then tramp around the old wharves and buildings. There were some wonderful places all huddled together that must have been mediaeval, and the names of some of the streets were marvellous, The Land of Green Ginger, for instance, off Blackfriargate. There was a fine Art Gallery where I spent some afternoons and revelled and rested my feet. I could not, and never have been able to, like the agonising pictures of Christ on the

Cross, and martyred saints. It made me wretched to think of God as anything but an all powerful beneficent love. I could not then associate love with agony, and fat goddesses, whose shape, by my own, I knew was absolutely wrong, I hated. Some nudes were lovely, and I fell in love with Rosa Bonheur's pictures. There were several fine ones there, of lithe, strong animals, full of beauty.

I found the public library too, and started to scan the advertisements for better class jobs, and straight away saw one which, in my impudence, I answered. It seems extraordinary, in these days, to think how few jobs there were. It was Thornton Varleys, the big highest class "store" in Hull, and for me to get in there was quite as hard as the well-known camel getting through the eye of the needle, but I lost nothing by writing, not even a penny stamp, for I slipped my letter through the letter box in the main door after closing time. They wanted a young lady as trainee for the managerial department. Among other things she had to be well educated, of good family and of exceptional character and appearance — me!

I said in my letter that I had been to Askwith village school and had been going on to Bradford, but that my mother was a widow now teaching at the Orphan Homes (I didn't say in the laundry) and that my father had been a vet, and that my appearance was good; no mention of laundries at all.

At the boarding house we had one weekly boarder who in my mind I always called Fluffy, I can't recall her real name. She had a well-to-do home some miles away to which she went at weekends, had been apprenticed to the millinery department at Thornton Varleys and was now a junior assistant in the department and was rather a silly little thing. Also I regarded her as "stuck up" as she ignored me. When I went in to dinner the next day there was a sudden hush, and I felt awful and wondered what I had done. Then Miss Lindsay said, "No, I think we ought to tell her and help her to get ready." It transpired that Fluffy had been told by someone in the office that the application of a girl who lived in the Girls Friendly Society Hostel was looked on with approval, and she was to be given an appointment for the next day. Stupefaction and incredulity were in their faces and all through dinner they talked about it; what did I say, how did it happen, and Miss Yates added, "Well, really, with such nice young girls of good family — can you imagine?" to all of which, knowing the lies I had told in my letter I returned a stupid, blank countenance. Miss Lindsay, bless her, said I must do them credit. My blue serge costume was nice and neat, she said, but she had a hat — and she flew upstairs and came down with a large-brimmed, softish straw hat, blue, and roused Fluffy up to find something to trim it with. Fluffy became quite inspired and found a wreath of large white and yellow daisies, and when I saw it I noticed my hair under the hat toned with the flowers above, and Miss Lindsay put her hand on my shoulder and said softly, "Spring, Grace." Fluffy found me a pair of white gloves and Miss Lindsay slipped a pair of lisle stockings round my bedroom door later that night. I polished my shoes till I could see my face in them, and

167

put a good pad of paper in the bottoms, for the soles of my shoes were getting painfully thin, and if it was wet, I didn't want the stockings to be spoilt. I went to bed with my head in a whirl and a feeling that it was all a myth, but in the morning the letter was on my plate. I was to see Miss Somebody in the managerial department for a preliminary interview at ten o' clock.

I remember nothing about the interview except that there were a great number of "young ladies" all round the sides of the waiting room, and I felt a sort of relief that of course it would come to nothing, but I and a few others after being seen were asked to come back the next day to see someone else. There was a definite atmosphere of hostility in the room this time, you could cut it with a knife, and one very well-dressed girl looked very hoity toity and superior, and I found myself hoping that at least she didn't get the job. I went through the dreaded door last but one before she did, to find a youngish man at a large desk, who looked kind, and after talking said Miss Somebody had been very impressed with me and he agreed with her, and would like me to come, but there was one more young lady to see, so would I go back into the other room and wait. I did and the hoity toity girl looked daggers at me as she went in. I didn't see her leave, but the young man, Mr Varley, said Mr Thornton would like to see me. I went into yet another room, where a quiet, severe looking man looked at me searchingly, talked a bit, again kindly, and then said they had decided I was most suitable for them, and they hoped I would realise what an honour it was to be trained by Thornton Varleys and would always put their interests first, and in view of the fact that my mother was a widow they would give me 7/6 a week instead of 5/- for the first year. He added that any parent in a position to do so would gladly pay for the honour of his daughter's coming to their store, but I should have a letter confirming the arrangement in the morning.

In the morning the letter I received was a formal note, asking me to call at eleven o' clock, and signed by Mr Thornton. When I saw him, he looked sorrowful. He had a letter in his hand. He said, "I have a disappointment for you. You may not know that in a large store like this, the important people are not the directors, but the shareholders, and the young lady who, with you, was considered most suitable to come into our managerial department is the daughter of a gentleman who holds a large number of shares in this firm. He has set his heart on his daughter coming in, and in every way she is suitable. I am afraid we must go back on our word to you, and take her." Of course I had known all along it couldn't possibly happen, and my face must have shown my hopelessness. Quite impulsively, for him, I should think, he produced something out of his pocket, and put a golden sovereign in my hand, "To make up for your disappointment, Miss Roberts," he said. I tumbled out and took my stony face back indoors at dinner time, and just said a shareholder's daughter had got the job after all. I think all but Miss Lindsay breathed a sigh of relief, for after all, what is the good of being a shareholder if you can't get the best things for your own children. You mustn't

169

go changing the existing order in this outlandish way. But she murmured, "Oh, the beast," under her breath, and as I passed her chair to go out after the meal, squeezed my hand hard.

So I went back to my wandering, and Mother said she would give me another week, then I must go back to the laundry man for a job as a laundry maid. In a few days the miracle had happened, and I was installed as a junior clerk — there wasn't a senior — in the highest-class shoe shop in the town, in Blackfriargate. I had written the same letter, told the same lies, and given Miss Tinniswood as a reference, and she sent a beauty, which the Manager gave me when I left. I did not like him from the first and was gauche and uneasy always with him. I was with the whole staff, if it came to that. He said if my figuring came up to my letter writing, it would do. The inside of the shop was a large oblong, and in the middle of the top half was a large wooden and glass box, divided inside into two. One half was my office, and the other was the manager's, with a door communicating. There was a rounded hole with a little shelf in the end of mine, where cash was handed in if any changed hands, but most of the business was on an account basis. I was given to understand the customers were all very wealthy people who had dealt with the firm for years, and nothing so indelicate as money was mentioned.

I can't remember the routine, or my duties clearly, they were never fully explained to me, and I never had a clear picture of the final result of the things I did. This, I think, is fatal to any young person, but I had to take sales slips handed in to me and enter various details from them into different books tabulated in different ways, not bookkeeping but an internal system of record-keeping organised by the firm itself. I had lots of other jobs as well, but at the end of the day everything I had entered on these different forms had to agree with one other sheet which I made from the totals. The Manager never explained to me what I was doing, merely called me names if everything did not come out right, which it did not at first try for quite a while. I think it was a very fine system of stock-keeping and sales but would have liked to have understood it. The Manager and one of the saleswomen kept the actual accounts. My first trouble came from the fact that I had hardly seen a telephone before, let alone used one. It was in the Manager's office, and it was not my duty to answer it really, but one early day when he and his "floozy" were at dinner, the salesman busy and the other saleswoman missing, it rang and rang and I could not ignore it. I picked it up as though it were hot, said "Manfields" as I had hear the others do, and was requested to fetch Mr So and so, so I put the receiver back on its hook, and went and fetched him. His remarks, when he found the line cut, nearly blistered the paintwork, as of course I hadn't asked who it was on the line. I was a fool and worse, but it didn't occur to them they had never told me how to use it. It turned out later in the day to have been Lady Somebody, who was most irate at being cut off.

The staff consisted of the Manager, a salesman, a quiet, deferential, efficient person who slipped around all day among his boxes and hardly ever spoke except in a soft, genteel voice to the customers, and two saleswomen, one a middle-aged, hard-seeming spinster, and the other, the "floozy". I never thought of her as anything else — oh, and of course the girl who came in each day and cooked us a dinner and prepared tea. She probably did cleaning as well. They all prepared from the first to put me in my place and keep me there. I noticed once again how people could have one voice and face for the public and quite another one in their private lives. I had only one, and would be asked who I thought I was, making myself out to be better than other people, this with many a slighting look at my shabby and down at heel appearance.

The manager and his "floozy" — I called her that in my mind since the day when Miss Hardacre, in a temper, called her so to me — sat together in his office quite a lot, and would often forget to keep their voices down, besides which "little pigs do have long ears", and I could not help learning a lot. He apparently had a wife at home dying of cancer and two boys. The Floozy was in the home quite a lot and just waiting to take over legally, and the two of them would say very bitter things about the poor wife. Like King Charles she took an unconscionable time a'dying.

I had been there about three months and was managing things pretty well, though it was not a happy place for me; I had been out for five minutes after having my dinner and went into my cubbyhole. All was quiet, and I assumed the Manager had gone to his dinner. Suddenly the first sound of the phone began, and as we were not supposed to keep customers waiting, I sprang to the door and opened it quickly to see the Manager just disentangling himself from the Floozy who was in an untidy heap in the corner. I fell out again, but of course they had seen me, and I them, and that was the end of that job. The rest of the week I could do nothing right, and on Saturday was given a week's notice.

Curiously enough, when I left he gave me Miss Tinniswood's letter of character. That was a blow, but quite soon I got another job, but at half a crown a week and my meals, as a junior clerk at a draper's shop with very long hours, and shut up all day in a small glass cubbyhole with my senior, in a stuffy, busy shop, generally full of customers and quite a large staff. There was just no air at all. Mr and Mrs Buckley kept the shop. He was a mean, slimy pious-seeming man and in the quiet times would talk religion in a superior way as though they had it all worked out, and she was a nagging, pious-seeming woman. The senior people lived in with the Buckleys and detested them. They, the staff, were a very decent crowd to work with, but work was the operative word. If they had gone round with whips they could not have got more out of us all. There was something horrible called "dissecting" which meant that every little price ticket had a letter on it which registered some type of stock, and that letter went on the bill, and we had to enter the letters of each sale on sheets so that the fluctuations in stock were noted. We gave change too, in those little balls which travel along wires, and either Mr or Mrs Buckley were there to say

"Come along, girl, don't keep the customer waiting, what do you think we pay you for?" Mrs Buckley also had the sex bug and was always trying to catch the men and girls out in misdemeanours, and spying round corners. She kept her eye on her husband too, and apparently not for nothing, for my nice little Miss North said "Be careful of the Old Goat, Grace, when I'm at dinner, and don't trust him nearer than you can help. He goes in for private knee pressing." They were nasty people, and I watched the papers for another job. But I think it was the lack of air that affected me, and I started fainting when I got up in the mornings.

Mother took me to the doctor, and he said, "Yes, yes, yes," and that when I wasn't working I must rest as much as possible and not rush about, but stay in bed till dinner time. This was impossible, of course, but I did what I could. At the hostel there was a big room in which a meeting was held on Sunday afternoon for the Girls' Friendly Society members, and I had been allowed to sit there and do my homework after supper when I was not at evening school, so now on Sunday mornings I sat there in a fairly comfortable chair and read. There were quite a lot of books of a fairly goody-goody variety around some shelves, but I found some I liked, particularly one by Conan Doyle called *The Stark Munro Letters* about a young doctor just starting on his professional career. I bought myself a copy later and it has been one of my favourite books, and I have often smiled at the difference in what a young man expects now and what he got then. I don't know how it got on those shelves.

My health didn't improve much and Miss Smith felt I was too much of a responsibility and asked Mother to take me away, so eventually Mother got permission to live out, and we rented a furnished room in a decent street for a while, but gradually went downhill as Mother just wasn't the type to live in a nice room and keep it nice, and I was not much at home. I think we had three different rooms in as many months, and then rented an unfurnished house, and started the bed and box business all over again. It was hard on Mother as she had been looked after outside working hours at the orphanage, and jolly hard on me as I too had been living decently, if unwanted, and had had a clean comfortable room to read and rest in for about eight months. From this house, which was in a mean little terrace near the orphanage and near open fields where I walked on Sundays, I had to walk about a mile and a half as I still couldn't afford to take a bus, and I think this was what caused my health to improve. I was sixteen in September, and soon after applied for a clerk typist's job and got it and left Buckley's. Here, at last, I attained the foot of the ladder of respectability that I had so fiercely, though probably unknowingly, been longing to reach. It was a real office job, in an office in Spring Bank, where my desk, in the window, overlooked the busy city life and yet was away up, out of the noise. I had 7/6d a week, and my hours were nine to six, and nine to one on Saturdays.

I was happy at evening school and pleasing the teachers and enjoying learning. I was getting to know the boys and girls, too, though they were all very much better dressed than I was, so I was all the more surprised when I found I had an admirer. He plodded the walk home behind me for a month before he plucked up courage to speak, and I couldn't really believe I wasn't mistaken in thinking he was following me. Unfortunately, though intensely respectable, he hadn't a word to say for himself, and had large mild brown eyes and a receding chin, and to myself I called him "Cow's Eyes". I was a stony-hearted young woman, and after a few months bored stiff with him, but had an awful job to shake him off. I used to think wistfully if only it had been one of the others, particularly a dark, curly headed youngster whose father was a bank manager, and who made up to me in class but ignored me outside.

During the summer only the shorthand, typing and book-keeping classes went on at the Technical College, but in September the other course started again and it was wonderful to be back in the big High School and to be among young people who remembered me, though there were, of course, a lot of new ones too. I try to remember myself during those months. I was a curious, shabby mixture of demureness and pertness, good appearance and shabbiness, and had a deep inferiority complex which I covered at times with too much noise, for I had rediscovered the tongue which had made Mrs White writhe, and could say innocent-seeming things to the geography teacher who couldn't put his stuff over, which made the others laugh, and made his job very difficult. He could only stand and slowly go very red, and stutter and I felt no end clever, silly idiot that I

176

was. The dark, curly-headed boy was there again, and sat next to me and made a lot of me till we got outside the school, when he melted away. His name was Harold Turner, but his friends called him Bill and I called him Billy. While he was just a nice, rather spoiled boy, and was quite ready to be on "spooning" terms with me when no-one saw, I wasn't having that. I was as proud as Lucifer, and when he first tried to put his arm round me said, "Why do you do that when you won't walk along with me?" He spluttered and stumbled and then burst out, "Well, look at yourself," and when I said I couldn't, said, "You're far too pretty, and yet you're not . . . you're not . . ." but he had no need to go further, once he realised I was not the spooning sort, I knew well enough. Not really respectable. Still, I liked him and we enjoyed a brother and sister relationship.

There is so much about those days and people that I remember. Hull was a big city with the New Town and the Old Town. The Old Town was, of course, round the docks, and people who had no business there kept away. Twice I heard my employer talking about it, once when a knife was stuck in a quite innocent stranger, and once when two men carrying wages had been attacked and robbed and one killed. The burden of their talk always was "the Government ought to do something about it", a refrain I seem to have heard all my life.

The New Town had been very well planned, on American lines, so I was told, and the long straight streets, so different from the twisting narrow ones of the Old Town, went straight out from the central square like the fingers of a hand from the palm. There were fine new stores and shops and railway stations and libraries and Post Offices and the Art Gallery and churches.

The only time I have ever seen a Roman Catholic street procession was in Springbank, and it was quite as impressive to my simple mind as those I have seen since in continental countries. There seemed to be as many gold vestments and images and caskets there as I saw in Portugal years later and the beautifully coloured image of the Virgin and Child made me want to cry.

I had started attending the Presbyterian Church as soon as I got to Hull, partly because it was near the Girls' Friendly Society, and partly, I'm afraid, because I wanted something as different from the Misses Yateses' religion as possible. I joined the choir, but otherwise no-one took much notice of me except to move their skirts a little nearer to themselves when I sat nearby. One day the Minister asked for helpers for a mission which was on the fringe of the Old Town, so I volunteered, and went there every Sunday afternoon for quite a while. The man who ran it was the most unsuitable, ineffective man possible for the job. Apart from the small children, it was attended only by hefty great louts who came for the simple pleasure of making a fool of him, and every now and then tearing up or smashing everything in sight. There was another girl and myself helping him, and I can't for the life of me remember anything we did of the slightest use. We huddled with some tiny girls behind a kind of partition, while Mr Gordon, wearing his bowler hat (from which he never parted), popped up and down like a male Aunt Sally at a fair, dodging a hail of hymnbooks and even harder missiles, the while imploring the dear-r-r lads to remember the blessed Lor-r-rd Jesus who came to save them. And when we left, they always gave us a sporting start, and then followed us with a hail of half bricks and stones and their "just misses" were very well-placed indeed, and the bowler sailed off sometimes.

In those days, I think, a great many worthy but incompetent people spent much of their lives trying to help the poor in entirely wrong ways, and doing more harm than good. The other helper was my first friend in Hull, a girl named Tottie, and I loved her. I suppose she had another name but I can't remember it. She was about two years older than me and she was very pretty, with curly auburn hair and green eyes, and one of those real pink and white complexions and a sweet little retroussé nose. She also had a large stuck-out mole on the side of her chin, with several long ginger whiskers sticking out and she was very conscious of it. She was the most merry, jolly little person imaginable and taught me to laugh at a great deal of life and to see the funny side of things — a thing I hadn't done much before, being always taken up with the beauty of things around, the undesirability of my position, and the thinness of my skin. She was a real tonic, bless her. She was better placed than I was, but not too much. Her father had been the manager of a shop but lost his job, and they had come down, and were living as caretakers of some offices with a flat in the basement.

Tottie didn't go out to work, but helped her mother pretty well full-time in the cleaning. She was very good for my ego, as she told me I was very pretty, that they all thought so including her brother, so ladylike and clever. I was never easy with this brother. He was sharp-looking, tall and dark, quite intelligent, and in these days would have been a communist. He was all for a good revolutionary upheaval. I don't see how any thinking man at the bottom could have been otherwise then, but he refused to talk politics to me. He had a very poor opinion of girls, except for amusement. He and Tottie had lots of arguments about me, I found out later, and one night had a bet that he could easily make up to me and get me to kiss him. I was surprised when he dropped his cynical kind of manner and asked me if I would like a walk in the fresh air. I said, "Yes, rather," expecting Tottie to come too, but she said she must help her mother, so feeling very awkward I went out in the dark back streets with him, and we walked along in dead silence. He asked if I would like some sweets, and I said, "Yes, thank you," so we stopped at a little general shop and bought some toffees. For once he had nothing to say, but I wanted some intelligent conversation. Knowing that in his otherwise empty head was the fact that Hull hadn't an Association Football team, only a rugger one, which was a fearful insult to the workers, but knowing nothing whatever about football, I rummaged in my mind for things I had heard him say and managed to get him going, from football to local civic affairs to national politics, and we walked on and on, chewing toffees and talking our heads off. We

180

arrived back considerably later than we had been expected. He must have forgotten all about the bet, for I saw Tottie lift her eyebrows and say "Well?" and he went as red as fire and looked extremely silly. She told me about this some time afterwards.

Poor Tottie, she was eighteen, and girls were expected to marry and take themselves off their parents' hands. They thought it was unnatural that she and I should enjoy each other's company so much and go for long walks together on our rare free afternoons. Before very long they were encouraging a tall thin man with a droopy moustache to pester her for her company. She laughed and made fun of it at first, after all he was thirty, quite elderly, but his persistence and her parents' pressure won in the end and we had a solemn talk and parted. They showed me very plainly I was not wanted, and goodness knows what they said to her. She gave me a volume of Milton's poems which had always been a great treasure to me. She was bright enough, and had not had any interest in books and poetry, but I would talk to her by the hour as I had never talked before, and I would absolutely glow under her appreciation, and she would talk about the dressmaker's business she longed to have, to get away from home and never touch a scrubbing brush again, and not having the clerks slapping her on her plump little behind as she knelt down. She had a figure rather like Queen Victoria's. We helped each other a very great deal.

I also made another friend and kept her until I left Hull. As I have said, I was very conscious of the fact that I was not so well-dressed as the other girls, and never made any advances to them, but was astounded in the Christmas holiday to receive, by post, an invitation to a party at a private house from a tall fair girl named Hilda Rhodes. I wrote straight away, without permission, accepting, and then had some wretched days while Mother insisted I was not to go. The poor soul was very lonely, for I left her alone a great deal in the evenings, but I blundered ahead like a bulldozer at that time, battering at every thing that stood in my way of improving myself. I went, promising to be home by twelve, and I was too, and the Rhodeses thought all the more of me for obeying my Mother.

They were a completely new side of life to me. They lived in a nice semi-detached double-fronted, bay-windowed house in a good road off Beverley Road. There was Mrs Rhodes and her old mother. The eldest son, Carl, was articled to a solicitor. The other son pined to be a musician, and shut himself up in the sitting room most of his spare time playing the piano, but he wasn't trained as his father said one musician in the family was enough. He was training as an engineer. There was also an older sister, large and dark, who was a teacher. Mr Rhodes was the conductor of one of the famous opera companies who toured about most of the time, and I never saw him at home. The family talked so little of their father that I have often wondered whether perhaps this was not an irregular establishment, without benefit of clergy. There was sufficient money, but not too much, but certainly a higher standard than I had ever pictured myself sharing in.

Hilda was seventeen, a few years younger than Carl, and her position in the household was that of the younger daughter, a little petted but not too much, whose job it was to stay at home and help Mother for her keep and a little pocket money. She had been told she could invite one nice girl, rather on the "someone for you to play with" lines, I think, and thought of me straight away, perhaps because I was so ladylike and they would approve.

There were about half a dozen pairs and Hilda and I were suitably quiet and shy, I think, but inside I was in the seventh heaven. At half past eleven the elder son had to take me home, and for a blissful twenty minutes or so I talked intelligently, or tried to, to an intelligent man, and he told his mother I was a well informed young person, and would make a good friend for Hilda.

After that I went to tea pretty well once a week, always in the back room with the women. I never mixed with the young men again, though I saw them, god-like, in the background. I think mothers took great care their sons should not meet young attractive girls if they could help it, so the fiction was kept up that Hilda and I were children. But Hilda was no child, and had already decided she was going to marry a young friend of Carl's. He didn't know it but she did, and in the meantime she was determined to have freedom from home surveillance occasionally, and that was where I was useful. Her mother and brothers approved of me, they accepted my story of my background — my Mother was a widow, a matron at the Orphanage; that was quite respectable, and made it quite correct for them to send their regards sometimes but not to ask her to visit, as she would have no spare time, and my sisters were living together in London as business girls. Rather advanced, but understandable in the circumstances. So whenever there was something Hilda wanted to do, I had to ask if she could visit me. Mother would have been very surprised to hear how many times she took us to the park to listen to the band — something forbidden to the decorous young as the boys and girls milled round and round and had no other objective than pairing off, often with complete strangers, but with my Mother, of course, it was quite airtight.

I remember once Mother was allowed to take us to a fair, and we were "picked up" early in the proceedings by two young soldiers, parted company and didn't meet again for a couple of hours, though we caught sight of each other occasionally on the round-a-bouts or swing boats, or something. To my chagrin Hilda grabbed the taller of the two, leaving me with a shortish, thick set, silent lad who was, I think, as embarrassed as I was. I didn't feel comfortable at his spending money on me, and we did a lot of walking round looking at things, but apart from feeling guilty it was all very exciting with the blare of noise and the lights. The boy behaved with great propriety, and when we did eventually meet with the other two, with their arms round each other, were laughed at for being solemn old stick-in-the-muds. Hilda there was very different from Hilda at home. Of course, for this deception I had to describe Mother minutely so that she could talk about her to her family, and I never let on that we were not still living in the

184

respectable house that I had been returned to from the party.

We were still buying clothes through the Exchange and Mart, and I was getting good at altering them to fit me, though my stitches would never bear inspection, but when I look back it is incredible how little things cost. Stockings were sixpence a pair, ribbons a penny and two pence a yard; I remember buying two pretty hats at sixpence each at a sale, and my shoes never cost more than 4/11d a pair. Of course they were not good and did not last, and soling and heeling cost 1/-, so more often than not mine let in water badly and were stuffed with paper. I remember the mortification of walking along among people and feeling the paper wad working up out of the side of my shoe, also the dreadful knowledge that there was a large hole in the heel of my stocking. For a while one could hide it by taking off one's shoes and pulling the stocking down and doubling it over one's toes, but gradually the stocking slipped back, and the hole was visible once again.

I think it was early in 1914 that I started to work for Mr Lewis. He was an insurance and commission agent, which meant that he gained admission to poor people's homes by selling them small insurance policies and collecting their premiums, but carried with him a case containing trays of jewellery and watches, which he sold to them at so much a week. He was an intensely respectable man, a pillar of the church, and was much looked up to by the well-dressed friends who occasionally came into the office, though he did not spend all that much time in the office. My job was to

185

keep the insurance books up to date, marking up the premiums paid, and the books with names of the buyers of jewellery and their weekly payments, and occasionally typing a letter or different lists of stock, nothing very arduous, and the hours from nine to six seemed very lonely and long in that first floor room all by myself. Also, if I wanted to go to the lavatory I had to go downstairs through an office where a grinning, fair young man sat who always seemed to be making fun of me, through a tiny back yard to a beastly, filthy little privy like those of my childhood, only worse, because it was hemmed in with buildings, and more used.

When he was in the office I found my employer intensely dull. He was a most worthy person and surprisingly good-looking, and when sitting in his chair looked broad and tall, but his legs must have been short and out of proportion, for when standing or walking he looked short, and was, I imagine, shorter than me which made him most uninteresting so far as I was concerned — such a pity, for some of his men friends were nice and tall, and quite oncoming when he wasn't looking. Then he gradually thawed, and talked to me about his parents, who were dead, and his brothers and sisters who he had more or less supported for some years, though they were off his hands now, and his youngest brother who he had sent to Winchester and who had died the previous year of diphtheria, to his great grief. He was a simple, stiff sort of man who seemed to have had no real life of his own, only church and work and money making. He was a strict Tory, and had very decided opinions about the place of the "working man" in the community. He asked me what I thought about his commission agency, was there any harm in selling jewellery on credit to these women when their husbands were away at sea? They couldn't have brooches and watches if they had to pay cash for them, and he thought he was doing them a favour, and yet a great hulking fellow who had come home unexpectedly had threatened him with violence if he came near the place again, and he, of course, was half a crown a week short on repayments, yet it stuck out a mile to me that half a crown was a large part of the money the seaman was able to give his wife for the children's food when he was away at sea. Yet of course I couldn't tell him so, and he couldn't see it for himself. It was just another proof of the iniquity of the working classes.

I remember quite distinctly when his attitude to me changed. Jessie did an unprecedented thing, and sent me a discarded coat of hers that was still quite good. It was a golden brown astrakhan with a nice, slim tailored line, and as my colouring was golden, it suited me very well. One of my sixpenny hats was golden brown too, a soft woven straw with a brim, and I had trimmed it with a darker brown ribbon gathered into a pompom at the side. At six o' clock I went into our second room — we only used it to put our hats and coats in — put on my "new" coat and hat, smoothed myself down, patted my hair, which fortunately curled, and wondered if Mr Lewis would notice the difference as I went back through the office. He never came in until after lunch so hadn't seen my transformation. He glanced up to say a casual "goodnight" and stiffened in his chair as though someone had jabbed him with a hatpin, and his fine grey eyes nearly popped out of his head. "You beautiful golden girl," he said, and then went pale and stiff and apologised, but then asked what I had I done to myself. I explained it was merely a new hat and a new, old, coat my sister had sent me, and I said goodnight and fell outside. I must have looked quite nice, though, as I had a full-bloodied wolf whistle from the fair-haired boy downstairs, who was putting up the ground floor shutters as I went through the door.

Poor Mr Lewis never recovered; it was such a shame he was so short! He started spending a little more time in the office and started conversations, obviously wishing to find out what I was like inside, and what my interests were, poor man. From my dustbin at Felsted I had read more books than he had ever heard of, and as for politics, I had talked so much to every worthwhile old or young man I had ever met about the iniquities of the System he so much believed in, I could have laughed aloud at the pompous platitudes he uttered — but of course I didn't. I thought of him as quite an elderly person, and was polite. I don't know what the rate of Income Tax was at that time, but he thought it utterly iniquitous, and the National Insurance Act, the Ninepence for Fourpence, was wicked. The working man would bring the country to ruin. The only sensible thing to do was to conscript all the young men who were out of work, and put them in the Army, for a war with Germany was inevitable, and then we would be ready. Let them get on with the unpleasant things, leaving worthwhile people to their stocks and shares and their big wholesale businesses, and to keeping Britain powerful in trade. It wasn't the soldiers and explorers who had made the British Empire what it was, gadding around the world looking important, it was the business man who stayed at home and invested his money and made it earn more. Then I think he began to get "cold feet", for one morning I went in to find my table and chair with the few books and box files had been moved into the little back room, and for a week I sat and froze all by myself. It was about February or early March, and we had no heating in either room, no electric fires then! His excuse was he might want to interview clients in his office, but though I was an ignorant girl I had more than once seen a look on his face that I didn't like, and thought to myself that I hoped he wasn't going to be silly, and I sensed that though for some reason he now liked having me with him, he was also scared that he might DO something that would not be wise or good, and he was essentially a very good person. Thank goodness he preferred me in with him, and I found one morning quite soon, my bits moved back.

One Saturday I found a very small packet of chocolate on my desk after he had gone, and then Easter came and he presented me with a pound box of chocolates, the first I ever had in my life. He had his bowler hat in his hand as he gave them to me and said he hoped they would make my weekend more pleasant, and his hand touched mine and his face went all white

189

and stiff, and he jammed his bowler on and almost fell over his feet going out of the door. And I, silly embarrassed little idiot, stood and giggled as I watched him cross the street below.

Apparently he still didn't trust himself alone with me and after Easter we had an addition to our small staff, a middle-aged ex-sea captain, whose wife had decided she couldn't live alone while he was away at sea — she had two children, eight and tennish, so I couldn't see where the loneliness came in — but he left the sea and came, temporarily, to get new connections for us, lugging round a bag of jewellery and tempting the lower class housewives to buy a gold watch or brooch at so much a week. I can't remember if he was much good as a salesman, but I detested him. He was one of the smarmy type, yet overlaid with a bluff honest sea-dog manner, and while we checked over together the contents of his bag and the figures in his book, would manage to be my side of the desk, and his hairy hands always seemed to be straying and touching me somewhere or other, and his voice would go all "coo-ey". I was very unsure of myself, and thought it was my imagination and an unhealthy mind, and while feeling most uncomfortable, and squirming as far away from him as I could, put up with it. After all, he only came in twice a day, to get his bag in the morning and to report and check up in late afternoon, soon before Mr Lewis came in, and I hoped to heaven he would leave us soon. And he did.

My employer arrived in the middle of one of his most oppressive leaning over acts when I was really quite frightened; his hand was on my knee while he breathed whiskey all over me and told me he had been "celebrating" with a couple of shipmates he had met by chance. I was always terrified by the smell of alcohol, and must have looked it, for in a few minutes I was asked to go down to our wholesale jewellers on some small errand — they were not far away, and I loved going, firstly to get out in the air, and then because two of the young men there were tall and fair and pleasant, and had been rather jokey and fun until this last month or two, when they had gone all solemn. When I got back to the office Mr Foster had gone and he didn't come back again.

Mr Lewis had started lending me books, and started off with *The Bride of Lammermoor*, which he said he thought really good literature, so I riposted with *Vanity Fair*. I think perhaps he hadn't got any more books, but having got going I lent him several of H G Wells's novels — if Mother had only 6d in the world and saw a dog-eared novel for 2d she would buy it, so we had quite a few around. These shook him rather, I think, and I just about finished him off with a book by, I think, Robert Erskine. I can't remember the title, but it was about a man — a priest — who thought too much and became an agnostic and then an atheist. Of course he put it all right by dying and regaining his faith on his deathbed, but it had stimulated me and made me think. I had, by myself, worked out a faith in my childhood that suited my circumstances. As a matter of fact, I don't think I could have survived without a simple, but real, belief in Jesus, the son of God, who loved ME, but

191

now that I was gradually sloughing that old skin of real poverty and growing a little more, though very little as yet, of the soft fur of respectability around me, I am afraid I began to question the love of God in the light of the inequalities I saw around me, and I was seeing very clearly that all was certainly not for the best in this far from best of worlds, and that the Being in charge of it all did seem to turn a blind eye to a great many things that would have done with being investigated. Mr Lewis's simple Presbyterian faith was that as long as you made as much money as you could, paid your rates and taxes — which you hoped would be kept as low as possible — did your duty to your family and to a lesser degree to your neighbours — those people you knew who were in the same income bracket as yourself — well, the rest of the people were not your concern. There were workhouses and orphanages paid for out of your money for people who had been unfortunate, and casual wards for the lazy louts who wouldn't do regular work. So my novel about a renegade priest who questioned the natural order of Society, following it up with leaving his wealthy living and going to live in the slums and spending his own small income on out-of-work prostitutes just was beyond his comprehension. I don't think he tried to read far into it, but brought it back, and we didn't pursue literature further.

CHAPTER
FIFTEEN

Mother and I had rather a bad time just about now. When she became reconciled to Doff and Edith living in London she apparently made quite a thing of their going once a month or so to visit Florrie, our epileptic sister who was at an asylum near Dartford in Kent. This, of course, was a big expense for them, besides being most heartbreaking and unpleasant. How unpleasant I did not know until Mother told me quite casually one morning that I was to meet a certain train, from which Florrie was to be handed over to me as she was coming to live with us. As Florrie left us when I was about three, after the bad biting episode, she meant nothing but a name to me, and I imagined I would be meeting a little girl, instead of which a uniformed nurse came to be dragging a short, fat woman who might have been any age. She had a large loose fat face and a hanging, sagging mouth, and large glasses with very thick lenses which distorted her eyes. She wore a hideous hat, and bulky, thick, long coat, and large thick shoes which I have always thought of as "institution shoes". She looked an idiot, and was obviously terrified. The nurse said in loud, artificially cheerful tones "This is Bobbie, your sister. You remember her, don't you? Be a good girl," and dumping a pitiful paper parcel at my feet, departed in the direction of the station buffet. Poor Florrie made a movement towards the back of the nurse, something that she knew, but I made myself put my arm round her shoulders, when she crumpled up a bit and mumbled "Bobbie, love Florrie," and I held her hand, she picked up the parcel and hugged it, and we went out of the Paragon Station to the bus, which fortunately took us all the way to our little road.

She was frightened of all the people in the bus and along the road, I don't suppose she had been out in a street since she had been put in the asylum, a girl of nine or ten; she was now about twenty-four. To her the Asylum ward was home and safety, and the people around her, however unbalanced they were, and however dreadful they looked, were the familiar and the known. Mother had, on rare occasions, had periods when she spoke of Florrie a lot, and she was always saying how pretty she was, and how nice, except for her dreadful temper when she had a fit, and we had a photograph of two little girls, sweet little things, with round faces and large eyes and beautiful curls — Florrie and Dorothy, and that was what I had always had in mind when she was mentioned, and that was what had grown up in a ward full of idiots in one stage or another of madness, until she became like them, a heavy, scowling, slow-moving, sub-human lump. When we reached our house, where I had prepared some mild sort of a meal, I managed to part her from her outdoor clothes and we sat down to eat, but she was so excited

194

and wanted to cling to me all the time, and she shovelled food into her mouth and slobbered and spilt it all over the place. She couldn't make conversation, but kept saying single words I couldn't understand and then got angry and stuck out her great bottom lip, and her distorted eyes sort of glinted at me through those great lenses; I could not help thinking of an angry pig in Mr Saville's sties. And here, in this house, she was going to be alone each morning and afternoon, and Mother, in her airy-fairy way, had said, "She'll be able to have your dinner ready for you each day." I was due back at the office, as I had only asked for the morning off, and did not know what to do, but she solved it by sitting in our one and only old armchair with her precious parcel, and going to sleep. Looking back it seems a dreadful thing to have done, but I really was scared nearly out of my wits. I grabbed my outdoor clothes, scooted out of the door, locked it, and ran for the bus back to the office. Mother had said she would come home early, and I thought, thank goodness, she can take the responsibility of her.

I was too optimistic. When I got back home, after having had a couple of hours evading a very worried employer's questions, I had told him an elder sister was coming home after a long stay in a hospital because she was now better, but he knew quite well there had to be something to account for my white face and worried looks — Mother was in the road waiting for me because she was afraid to be in the little house with Florrie, who was tramping restlessly from one room to another, up the stairs and down again, mumbling to herself all the time, and looking so wild and unhappy, poor thing. She was used to being caged in, but not in quite so small a place and certainly not by herself.

I think that evening I held her hand and sang our children's songs for several hours, and she was delighted and crooned with me, quite a sweet tuneful noise, while Mother raged and moaned alternately as to why the Asylum people had let her come home and how wicked it was, but if two intelligent, pretty, neat business girls who have visited an inmate once or twice produce a letter purporting to come from the inmate's mother, asking for said inmate to be sent home as she can now look after her, the overpressed hospital staff are going to be only too pleased to be rid of the inmate and are not going to ask too many questions. We went to bed early, and as we had only one double bed and no spare mattresses or blankets, it was three in a bed again. Florrie liked that, and snuggled down, but she moaned and muttered all night long, and once or twice jumped up in her sleep and tried to get out of bed, but we soothed her and she settled again. Mother's beautiful idea of Florrie tidying up and getting the dinner was of course a dream. We had to go out and lock her in the house, and she was a nightmare in my mind, morning and afternoon. Of course she had done nothing about dinner — she did not know how. At the Asylum she had done some very childish sort of job in the sewing room, like putting buttons of like sizes into the same boxes, and looping up lengths of tape, but nothing where she could possibly hurt herself. So for dinner we had to

196

find money for fish and chips and she walked to the shop with me and was so happy.

Naturally there was trouble when she found I was leaving her again, but I had to do it, and was worried stiff till I got back to her again. That evening we sang again, but she was getting restive and wanted to go out as she had seen me do. There was only one small room and a kitchen and she had been penned in all day, so Mother said she would be quite safe next morning if we left her in the garden. We could tie up the little gate, so after another more disturbed night, we pulled out the chair and some picture books into the garden, left the house backdoor open, and I tore away tying the gate behind me, hoping for the best, but I heard her roaring like the bull of Bashan by the time I reached the end of the road. I rushed home at dinnertime to find the garden gate open and the back door too, and no Florrie! I hurried down the road towards the Fried Fish shop, asking everyone on the way if they had seen her, then along in the other direction and round corners till I came to the fields, and there I found her rolling along, looking happy and crooning to herself. I had a job to get her to come home, and when we reached the streets she was getting noisy, and people stopped and looked at us, and someone asked if I wanted any help, and I wished the ground would open up and swallow me.

I don't remember what we did about dinner and other meals those few days. Probably we cooked something at the weekend and had some cold meat in the larder, but we couldn't leave Florrie much. She was as artful as a monkey at getting out and wandering off, and people in the few other houses in the road began to be very much aware of her, and look out for her, but be afraid to bring her home. They would hang about waiting for me to come in, and then say, "Your barmy sister's gone that way. Went hours ago. Something'll be happening to her if you're not careful," and then she would confound them by rolling along the road with one large smile all over her face and throw her arms round my neck. I don't know what made me feel worse, her slobbering caresses or the sly, squinting sullen looks and the muttering when she didn't get her own way. These began to get more frequent and more violent in a very short while, and it began to be obvious that she was working up for something. Her early affection for me disappeared, and she would say my name, following it with a stumbling string of oaths almost blood-curdling to hear. Perhaps we had become careless, but she found the scissors in the table drawer and sat half smiling with them in her hand, half opening them and twisting them towards me. Mother coaxed them away with a sweet or two she had, and she and Florrie went to bed, while I hid the scissors on the top shelf of the food cupboard.

We had a dreadful night that night. She muttered and then shouted, all about "Gimme knife. Knife. Cut froat!" and we had a job to hold her down in bed. She quietened and we, worn out, went to sleep, but I woke suddenly to realise she was not there. I jumped out, over to the narrow doorway. Mother had left the little night-light on, and there she was, coming up the stairs with something in her hand. I had read somewhere that

198

you must not wake a sleepwalker, so I stood back quietly. I don't think I was frightened for as the light fell on her face and her wide-open eyes, she had quite a sweet smile and her pretty hair fell round her shoulders, and she had our blunt carving knife in her hand. She stood at the foot of the bed where I had been lying, and smiled her squinting smile, she looked better without her glasses, and then quietly climbed round Mother into bed again, leaving the knife where I had been lying. I took the night-light and finished the night in the armchair downstairs, scared stiff.

I woke from quite a deep sleep to hear her bumbling about near me. It was 6.30 and Mother's little alarm had obviously gone off upstairs. Mother had to be at work at 8 and Florrie had dressed herself and was rooting about for her coat and hat, and was determined to go out. She seemed in an extraordinary state of violent excitement, and had we known anything about her condition, we would have known she was working up to some kind of attack and would have sought medical advice. Even in those days there must have been quietening drugs for people like her, but I knew nothing, and Mother was so worried and upset that she was hopeless. We had some sort of breakfast, but the cheap knives on the table seemed to have an unholy attraction for her, and she kept picking them up and stuffing them in her pocket — she still had her coat on — and both she and Mother kept fighting to get possession of them, and poor Mother got so upset, she just couldn't take it. Florrie kept grunting and snarling indistinguishable words, and when she wasn't grabbing

199

knives off the table she was pulling her hair down (she had lovely hair) or pulling at her great bottom lip, and we just didn't know what to do. We tried loving her and being kind, though we didn't feel like it, when what she was used to, I suppose, was discipline and great firmness.

Mother had to go, and I still had some time before I needed to go out, so, trembling and really frightened I tried to tidy up the room and bedroom and prepare something towards dinner. As Mother went, trying to slip out unseen, Florrie was quicker, and was out and down the path in a flash and went ahead of Mother along the road towards the fields, and I was so glad to see the back of her I made no attempt to fetch her back and neither did Mother. Anyhow, she was stronger than both of us, and would not have come, in that mood. I remember I sat down and cried and cried for quite a while, and then got up and made a half-hearted attempt to follow and find her, and must confess I was glad she was nowhere to be seen and told myself I hadn't time to go and look for her, but then I repented and went. I was late for the office anyhow, so I walked along to the fields, expecting every moment to see her ahead of me. I walked and walked along the familiar paths, but there was no sign of her and I realised she must have taken a different direction, so I retraced my steps back to the little roads around near our house.

It seemed hours I walked, though it wasn't, shrinking at every corner lest round it I should see the crowd that meant she had attracted attention by her manner, or had come to some harm and then I came back to our house again to see if she had returned, and to think what to do if she hadn't. I sank into the chair, and as I sat I heard her voice, distressed, hysterical. I flew to the door and opened it, and she was there with a policeman, with his hand on her arm, and he was oh, so kind and gentle. She was terrified and cowed. I am afraid the sight of his uniform awoke dreadful fears in her. He had a peaked cap, I remember, and she obviously associated him with the institution she had come from, and goodness only knows what memories and fears he had awakened in her poor bewildered mind. Her earlier belligerency had gone, she was dull, stupid and lost, and clung to me and would not let me go. The man sent away the people who had tagged along our little path, came in and shut the door and asked me to tell him all about it and not worry.

I told him our sorry story but not about the knives and explained why I was in charge and not Mother, and how I had searched for her, but in the wrong direction. He suggested I sat there while he made a cup of tea, and while we drank it he kept looking, first at Florrie and then at me, and then said, "And you say you are sisters. I just can't understand it." I explained that she had been shut up with nearly mad people for years and that that had altered her, and how she had apparently been a lovely little girl, and he nodded his head slowly, but then later still said "It doesn't seem possible." Then we heard a car, and he said it was arranged Florrie was to be taken where she could be cared for properly. Apparently she had more or less run amok in the main road quite near the Police Station, and it had been fairly easy for them to take her inside while they made enquiries around the small roads, where they were soon told where she lived.

Poor Florrie didn't want to get into the car, but he kept a firm hold of her arm — it had to be firm, I knew how strong she was — and sat between us for what was quite a fair drive, then through the big gates that still made my heart sink, they were institution gates, along a wide drive to large doors. And then poor Florrie began to fight as the driver opened the car door to help her out; she could see what was going to happen to her, and all the way into the building she screamed and shrieked and tried to get at me and do me some damage, for obviously in her mind I had brought her there and was responsible for her imprisonment. Once inside, her fighting turned to sobs, deep, inside sobs that tore at me and I went to comfort her, but she flew at me again and the kind policeman who was standing with me had to hold her off. And then two uniformed women with the harsh, false-kind voices appeared in the passage, took her, one each side and bore her off, dragging her feet in truculent silence.

I did not see her again for we never visited her. I suppose Mother had some communication about her from the Authorities, but she said nothing to me about it. She had been sentimental about her, on and off, for years, but now she had had the reality of her for a short while, managed to wipe her right out of her mind. Doff and Edith, to save themselves embarrassment, had had that poor soul taken away from the only friends and home she knew, to be with strangers who had neither the time nor the real wish to look after her. That was us, I mean.

The Asylum people had been so glad to get rid of just one inmate, they had taken a chance, and not troubled to find out if we were fit to have her or not. This is one of the really bad patches in my memory. I set it alongside the two poor cats at Weston. The policeman handed over some sort of form and was given another in return, a receipt for a parcel, I thought, but I could not think very straight, and he chatted cheerfully and pleasantly to the office staff, led me out again to the car and we drove off and that was the end of that. A very few years later Mother had a brief communication to say that Florrie had died of pneumonia.

I went back to the office, dinnerless, not quite sure what my reception would be, but my employer was kindness itself. I had a most extreme headache, and I knew my face was a ghastly colour, but finding I had had no meal he asked me if he could take me to lunch, but on my vehement refusal — I was far too conscious of my shortcomings to consent to dine in a public restaurant with a well-dressed man and far too proud to let myself down by looking so obviously inferior in company, he slid five shillings across my desk and suggested I went to the Kardomah and had a pot of strong coffee and perhaps a sandwich by myself, and make it last for an hour or so before I came back. And not a question did he ask. Short and old fashioned he may have been, but he was a kind gentleman. The coffee did wonders for me, and I found I was hungry and had two ham sandwiches and enjoyed them, and found the anonymity of the well-furnished good class restaurant, sitting among the well-dressed people, none of whom took the slightest notice of me, the best possible tonic. And, wonder of wonders, there was a pianist and a violinist over the other side of the room playing sweetish, mealtime sort of music. I think it was the first time I had heard a fiddle since the carol-scraping on the moors at Askwith.

Back at the office Mr Lewis was out and I worked quietly till he returned a little earlier than usual, and tried a little gentle probing as to the cause of my indisposition. I was quite an accomplished liar and coverer up, I am afraid, and told him my sister had been taken very ill again, and we had had to arrange for her to return to hospital without delay, and as he didn't know where I lived, I had not told him of our descent from the respectable furnished room in the good road to the tiny terrace house in our present grubby road, so he couldn't call around and make enquiries, which was a thing I rather dreaded. Mother was always hinting that he was fond of me, and I should encourage him, but though that was the very last thing I wanted, I hung on to the "genteel young girl" image I always put over, and could not have borne him, or anyone else for that matter, to know what my background really was.

We settled down again and soon poor Florrie was not even a memory. It was about June, I think, and the weather was delightful. Most Saturday afternoons Hilda and I went out together, and I dragged her down by the river and the wharves and the pier where the ferry came in from Immingham, and there were generally one or two fairly nice young men around who were only too glad to "pick us up". It was only a question of walking by the great wide estuary or on the pier, and being giggly and light-hearted together, but we were very young, and it was sunny and I was happy. I remember an evening outing, too, with Hilda. Her brother, the solicitor one, gave us two tickets to go on an evening trip down the river. There were probably fifty people or more on the ship, and we had a meal down below, and a band was playing on top, and as we sat or strolled and listened the moon came out and people danced, and to my silly mind all was romance. We didn't know any of the other people on the trip, but as Edward had given us the tickets, it was pretty obvious he did know some so we were quiet and demure, a solicitor's clerk's young sister and her friend.

These were the summer months before the "Great War", and as I look back I am sure there was a kind of excitement underneath everything. The talk was all of the war that was bound to come and of putting the Kaiser in his place, and the nice boys, there were about half a dozen of them, who were jolly and friendly to me, so long as their families didn't know, were on tiptoe with expectation all the time, just waiting for the word "go" which would permit them to join up. There was Billy, the cheeky, curly-haired bank boy who was "promised" to his cousin, and had to be held at arm's length because he really did get amorous at times, and his friend Frank. Going in to the Bank where they "worked", and where Mr Lewis had his account was most exciting then — I'm sure it is not such fun for young people nowadays. The staff was entirely male, of course. There was the long front counter, with five cashiers, each behind his brass railing, with the chief cashier in a sort of little sentry box at the end. Behind the counter, three rows of tall desks, and behind each one a clerk, generally a pink-faced youth, fairly fresh from school, each longing for a diversion from the interminable scribbling in passbooks and ledgers. Of course, there were not so many girls going in as customers then, most office work and consequent trips to the Bank were done by men. I would go through the door in a pleasurable flutter of excitement, though outwardly quite calm, and up would pop three rows of heads, and a gratifying chorus of wolf whistles would greet me, though before the Chief Cashier could emerge from his box, not a head was to be seen. He was a courtly little man with a twinkle in his eye, and always attended to me himself unless he was engaged, and made me feel as if I was the customer, with a large account, in credit. While he talked a little shower of closely folded pieces of paper and paper darts would come sailing over to land on the floor at my feet, or on the counter near me. The Chief Cashier never managed to see them, somehow, and I was generally able to salvage some of them and squeeze them in my hand, to be looked at outside as I walked back to the office — three xxx's on one, and "I luv you" on another — silly rubbish, and no clue as to whom they were written by, but very heart warming.

206

I never had the courage to join the Parade, though I longed to. This took place every Sunday, summer or winter, wet or fine, in just one street off Spring Bank. I don't remember its name, and it seemed as though at five to four there was not a young thing to be seen, and at four o'clock the pavements were full to overflowing with couples — two girls or two boys. The girls all wore their best clothes and looked quite charming, and of course knew it. In the spring there were lovely new outfits and each tried to outshine the others. I think it was as much a fashion parade in the first few weeks as the girl pairs stopped to discuss and to finger each other's frocks and admire their hats with squeals of laughter and high-pitched remarks, but always with one eye on the youths on the opposite pavement. The object of the exercise was to pair off, of course, but they took their time over it, and when a boy and girl had taken the other's eye and summed up each other's points, a great deal of detective work went on behind the scenes before they stepped off their pavements and joined the mixed couples in the roadway. Then as the longer evenings spread out, if the affair was really "on" the young things went on to the Park to listen to the band, and as the dusk fell to wander off through the gardens and the shrubberies. I often listened to the band in the Park those lovely summer evenings in 1914. Even if one was alone there was great pleasure in being one of a crowd of happy people, watching the families and the paired off couples, and listening to the Strauss waltzes and the military marches which made up the programmes.

207

But then on two consequent Sundays I saw Mr Lewis in the crowd on the other side of the Bandstand, and melted away in the opposite direction as quickly as I could, for he had a lady with him, and the last thing I dared face was one of his sisters picking me to pieces. I don't think he saw me the first time, for he did not say anything about it, but the second time he said, "My sister and I saw you last night in the Park by the Bandstand, but then you disappeared." I looked blank, and said, "Oh how strange," or something equally feeble, and kicked myself mentally for having inadvertently let it out that I occasionally spent my evening that way. Then he asked me stiffly one day if I would care to go to the pictures with him — there was one of those big spectaculars, *Ben Hur* or something — at the big Picture House, but I mumbled something about my mother not allowing me to accept invitations like that, so later in the week he put two tickets on my desk for two seats in the Balcony, and said would my mother and I do him the honour of accepting them. Do him the honour, indeed. Mother saw me already comfortably married, and herself with a prosperous son-in-law, and if she could would have pushed me through his front door and followed herself. She told me I was to play my cards right and not be a silly fool and he would marry me, and I looked at her and thought of all I knew about her and her life, and thought of him, old enough to be my father, narrow-minded, old fashioned, kind and . . . very SHORT . . . and felt sick.

Our seats were high up, towards the back of the Balcony on one side, and at some period when the lights went up I saw Mr Lewis on the other side, lower down and rather hemmed in. There was a Ladies' cloakroom not far behind us, and I very quickly slipped out of my seat and in through the door, telling Mother I felt sick. I didn't go back until the lights had gone again, then, just before the end of the big picture, I said I just must go, I felt bad again, and most reluctantly she came out with me, and that encounter was avoided. She didn't know that he was there, of course, and he didn't mention it to me. I got in first and said that Mother thanked him very much and we had both enjoyed the film, and that was all. I felt for some weeks that he was trying not to be too friendly to me and the weekend sweets stopped for a while.

Then through July all the talk, suddenly, it seems, was of war. None of the older people wanted it, yet it is curious how inevitable it seemed. Mr Lewis had a very long face, and talked about how bad it would be for trade and the price of gilt-edged, and how shares would drop. All the older people, while insisting that Germany must be stopped, equally insisted that it was a matter for the professional soldiers — that's what we pay them for — and that ordinary young men should stick to their counters and their desks and work harder to pay for the war. We young people, without responsibilities and without the remotest idea what war really meant, were wild with excitement, though when August 4th came, and war was really declared, this was overlaid with a kind of solemnity, a responsibility; we felt this was something we ordinary young people had to fight to stop, this trampling down of weaker people by the strong. Billy and Frank were going together, and Dick and Steve from the Insurance Office, and each day one heard of brothers and sons who were "joining up". Of course, lots of parents managed to hold their young sons back for a while — it wasn't worth throwing up a good job when the war would be over by Christmas — Hilda's brother Carl was mad to go but was held for a while by paternal edict, while Edward sat tight in his solicitor's office.

After the first rush of joining up, it seemed as if they were not wanted, for the boys hung around the streets half the day and would gather in knots "chi-icking" the girls, their last bit of real freedom, but one evening just as I was clearing up my desk, there was a knock at the door and Billy came in. He stopped dead on seeing Mr Lewis, who glared at him, but as it was six o'clock I said, "I'm coming now," put on my hat, picked up my gloves which I carried because they were past mending, said "Goodnight, Mr Lewis" and walked out. When we got outside he explained that he had thought the "old man" had gone, as he couldn't see him when he looked up at the window. He was very excited, and I knew something must be going to happen as he had never come upstairs before. His usual thing had been to hang about over the other side of the road watching for me, when he would cross and walk me part of the way home. The news was that next day all of the recruits were to gather at some unearthly hour, march round the city, gathering up men at different points, and then be transported to training camps, goodness knows where. There was no cloud in his sky, he was perfectly happy. I asked him what Jess thought about it, did she mind, to which he replied, "Why should she mind? Someone has got to do the job, and anyhow, it would all be over by Christmas." And then he said, "I shall write to you. Will you write to me?" and I assured him I would, and as we shook hands, two very good friends, and said "Au revoir", I was so very, very thankful I was not in love with him. I could have been, easily, but his honesty about Jess and his fun had kept our friendship on a sound basis. He did write to me, frequently, for more than two years, and I answered. Only too soon his letters were censored ones from the trenches, but the last one was uncensored. Someone had brought it out for him, obviously, and it was terrible that a young man of twenty-one should be brought to such a state of mind. He tried to tell me of the misery of the conditions in the trenches, of the filth, the water over their boots, of the rats and the stench. Of the constant roar of the guns, of the death and fear all around, and of the stupefying and deadening knowledge that certain annihilation would be the end for them. I answered this, of course, but it was the last letter I had. I heard no more.

Next morning I could not give my mind to my work, I was watching and listening all the time, and at about ten o'clock I heard music and the sound of marching. I ran over to the window and looked down Spring Bank as they came into view, marching evenly and well in their civilian suits, each wearing an armband, and most wearing either cloth caps or bowler hats — not many bare heads in those days. As I picked out Billy's curls on the outer rank he looked up and waved to me, and I saw so many young faces that were familiar to me, among whom was "Cow's Eyes" marching bravely with the best of them. Crowds had gathered on the pavements and cheered and waved, and marched along with them to the station and there were Union Jacks galore, but it was obvious that there were very many heavy hearts in the crowd. As for me, I stood with the tears running down my face, though I think it was mostly rage and pity for myself being a girl, tied to the dull, daily round of this office, instead of going off into the blue like these glorious young men, doing deeds of incredible bravery for England.

Yes, when I was young we did think like this, and we meant it. It has taken that war and another war to disillusion the present young generation. Mr Lewis came in as I stood there, as they still went past. He had apparently been in the fringe of the crowd, watching. "Silly young fools," he said. Then later he asked me if the young man who had come upstairs meant anything to me. "He is a very good friend," I replied. "He is down there, one of those." My memory tells me that from now on an unnatural quiet hung over everything. The trams didn't seem to rattle and bang along Spring Bank as they normally did, and there were not so many. The pavements were emptied of their cheerful, cheeky young men, and the young men who were about seemed to go along quietly, as if avoiding attention instead of attracting it.

Evening school seemed so different, so many more girls and younger boys, and more women and older men among the teachers, and the whole atmosphere was different. And one thing I always remember, is the noise of the ships on the river and in the estuary, talking to each other all night long. The first night after war was declared, as I lay down in bed, I was aware of many, many ships, all communicating with each other by means of their hooters, sirens and bells. They had been there, going backwards and forwards all the time I had been in Hull, bringing goods in and taking goods out, but presumably in a full blaze of light where they could see each other and I was not aware of them, but now, unlit on the dark water, their warning notes came over the sleeping city, and the reflected glow which I had loved to watch from our little window was dead. We knew nothing of Air Raids, threatened invasions, or any of the things which came later, but the continuous noises from those ships, coming through the dark night, gave me a comforting feeling of safety, none the less for being quite a false one.

As the weeks passed I remember the news of our "First Hundred Thousand" being scattered and the papers were full of stories of German atrocities. One day I went down the narrow stairs to go outside to the privy, scuttering past the office door opposite which the fair boy sat, but he caught me, and his face was pink, for a change. "I'm going," he said. "My old folks have agreed. I wouldn't go till I'd talked them into it." I said tartly — and unkindly — "Why bother?" He went redder than ever. "Have you seen the papers lately.

They're killing old people and cutting girls' breasts off. Girls like you. How would you like that? They've got to be stopped, and I couldn't live with myself if I didn't go and do my share of trying to stop 'em." He looked as if he thought he could stop the whole German Army in one mad rush. As I escaped to the back door he called out, "I'm going on Monday, so it's goodbye." A girl was in his seat in a few days, but it was not the same.

CHAPTER
SIXTEEN

My birthday came at the end of September. I was seventeen, and quite grown up. I had worn my hair in ringlets — it had always curled — caught back with a ribbon, but now put it "up", I can't quite remember how, except that little curls at the back would escape and tickle my neck. Mr Lewis, it seemed, liked the ringlets, and screwed up his courage to ask me why I had altered it, to which I replied I must put it up as I was nearly seventeen. This brought the fact of my birthday out into the open, and he said he would like to give me a present, would I like a new dress. Why I really do not know, but I was both angry and humiliated, to think he thought I would want to accept CLOTHES from him, and I said "No", quite firmly. On being pressed I condescended to accept a neat little silver wrist watch on a leather strap — why on earth that was more respectable than a new dress, I don't know, but it was, to me, and I was most pleased with it. He asked if he could put it on my wrist, and as he did went all pale and stiff again.

In October wonderful things began to happen. Jessie wrote, telling me to have a photograph taken, and send a copy to her at once, and at the same time I was to let her know how far I had got in my business training. The photograph showed a demure young woman in a neat plain black dress with a sailor collar and striped vest; I had made it myself, by hand, of course, and if I had breathed very deeply, I think the stitches in the seams would have burst, but that didn't show in the photograph, and I was able to say with truth that my shorthand and typing were quite fair, my book-keeping very much more than fair, and my French medium, while my English knocked spots off everyone else's — I had a very good opinion of my capabilities by then. It then transpired that Jessie was going to marry her employer very shortly, leaving the flat which Dorothy and Edith had shared with her, that Edith was a most unsatisfactory and undependable person, and had been dismissed from her job at the Publishers and that I was to fill her place at both flat and office.

I was in the seventh heaven of delight and Mother was furious, but fortunately for me the Orphanage had to economise, because of the war, and Mother was given notice, and her assistant took her job without an increase in salary, and the orphans had to work a little harder. Mother had a month's notice this time, and I told Mr Lewis I must leave at the end of November, as we were all going to live together because of the war, and Mother was going to keep house for us! Then he started sending me out of the office to do all sorts of unnecessary jobs. First of all I went with a phoney sort of message to his elder sister, who offered me a chair, sat and looked at me for what seemed an age, and then produced a box and said, "Would I like a sweetie?"

216

Then soon I was sent to where he lived — a staid, neat, house, where I think he had "rooms", where he was coddled and "done for" by a middle-aged woman who adored him. I felt she looked down her nose at me very much, and didn't even ask me inside. Some other woman I visited had several charming children. She was a dear, and I think his sister-in-law. And we began to have quite a traffic through the office of tall, well set-up, prosperous, youngish and medium youngish men, all friends or relatives of his, and not one of them short. It did seem mean that he should be the only short one.

I couldn't get away from the fact that they had all come to have a good look at me, and very snooty one or two of them were. But his best friend, Mr Carmichael the wealthy jeweller, was polite and charming to me, and they stood and talked together at the top of the stairs. "Go ahead, Jack," Mr Carmichael said, "You marry a girl with money and her father thinks he's got the right to boss you for the rest of his life. And your wife thinks money's there to spend like water." Then they shut the door tight and went lower down the stairs and I didn't hear any more.

CHAPTER
SEVENTEEN

Things quietened down, the visitors ceased, and I had begun to think I had imagined the whole business, when one late afternoon, when he had sat for half an hour without a word, he suddenly turned to me — stiff and white again — and said, "Miss Roberts, will you be my wife? Will you let your Mother go to London with your sisters, and stay here and marry me? I swear I will do my best to make you happy." And his face came unfrozen and he looked all eager, and I just couldn't take it, and more or less burst out at him "Oh no — NO!" But having got as far as this, strangely, he didn't go all quiet again for long, and asked me if I cared for anyone else, to which I was able to reply honestly "No." Well, then, had I anything against him? How could I tell him he was far too short, far too old, and far too stuffy? I just couldn't, so I said "No" again. He then started talking as to how he had never thought about girls, not for himself. How he had been quite content seeing his brothers and sisters through, after his parents' death, and how he loved the youngest one, and when he died at Winchester, he had felt the bottom had fallen out of his world. How he hadn't noticed me much, at first, as a person, and then suddenly realised that instead of his mind being full of his young brother, it was full of me — he had put me in his place. And how he had tried to shut it out, I was so young, and then he had decided to wait for a year, and now I was going away. The words all came out in a torrent, and instead of being pale and stiff, he was red and excited, and twisted his chair round and leaned towards me. I suppose I looked scared — I know I felt it, and foolish and ashamed at the same time — but the mask came down again, and he said "You must not be afraid. You know I could never hurt you."

In a minute or two he put on his mackintosh, picked up his bowler, and still stiff and white stood and looked at me. "I'm afraid you have had a shock," he said, "I should sit for a few minutes, and then pack up and go home." He still stood there, looking, for quite a minute, with his hand on the door-knob, then opened the door and went through in one quick movement and ran down the stairs, and I saw him come out on the pavement below. And then, and only then, did I relax and lean my head on my desk and laugh — yes, laugh. I suppose it was partly hysteria, it certainly wasn't ridicule, but I had a feeling, why did it have to be him? Here was I, seventeen, all set for a tall bright young man nearer my own age to come a-courting, and what I got was a middle-aged man, at least six inches shorter than myself and as stiff as a poker. I did think the whole thing was exceedingly stupid. I didn't say a word to Mother, of course, though I know she waited daily for a momentous piece of news, but I jolly well wasn't going to give her the opportunity of telling me again what a fool I was.

Next day, before going on his rounds, Mr Lewis took some books and papers from his desk drawer, and put them on my desk, saying would I look through them while he was out. I thought they were insurance things, or something, for me to check, but to my intense surprise they were share certificates and all sorts of financial papers, which even to my inexperienced eyes showed that he had quite a substantial sum of money invested in all sorts of different ways, and that this insurance and commission business brought in only a small part of his income. I thought then that he must have conferred with Mr Carmichael, and that astute businessman had advised him that money would influence me in a way that he had not been able to. I thought "How stupid", and felt better over my own behaviour. I can't remember any more about him and the office, except the railway platform and the waiting train, and Mr Lewis emerging from obscurity as I stood at a window full of excitement, and he put into my hands a box of chocolates and a book. He wore his stiff face, and said, "Goodbye, Miss Roberts. I am honoured to have known you!" And the book, when I looked at it, was the war apologia, *A Scrap of Paper*! I don't remember who it was written by, but it was not light reading for a young girl on a railway journey. He stood on the platform as the train steamed out, a short, wide, stocky figure with his bowler in his hand, and Mother gritted her teeth and said "You silly little fool."

220

CHAPTER
EIGHTEEN

In London the four of us, Mother, Doff, Dith and me, lived for a short while in a three-room and kitchen flat in an ugly block of buildings in Islington. No bathroom or heating, of course, and a great deal of plain, cold concrete. The offer of Jessie's flat had been abruptly withdrawn as soon as Jessie knew that Mother was coming, and Jessie did not come near us. It was quite fifteen years before I even met her. We were all ostracised, really. The man she had married was very comfortable and had a couple of typewriting shops in the City, and a small chain of decent second-hand furniture shops, ending up with a stall or something in Caledonian Market, which he said was the most profitable of the lot. Anything that was too tatty to sell at the Angel or in Tottenham Court Road would be snapped up in the Market at twice its worth. They lived in a fine big house near Highbury Fields which had been a girls' school, and the old school hall was a fine place for him to store excess furniture. The girls told me the house was beautifully furnished with some of his best pieces. Unfortunately he had a way of bringing wealthier clients round to see these pieces if Jessie happened to be out, and she would return to find her cherished inlaid walnut table had been metamorphosed, and was now oak, or her Chinese rugs were now Axminster. But soon they would go and other choice pieces take their places.

We acquired a bit of furniture from somewhere, a deal table, four Windsor type chairs and two beds, and settled down. Mother was the world's worst housekeeper. She couldn't keep three nearly empty rooms clean, and as for her cooking, it could not have been worse. But she was a shrewd, keen woman, and in a week or so had been accepted by the Government as a Welfare worker-cum-overseer to the girls and women who had poured into Woolwich Arsenal. She volunteered for permanent night duty and was, of course, exceedingly well paid for the first time in her life, and she had quite a position at the factory, and enjoyed it. She slept all day and travelled or was in her office all night, and I was back at my old job of keeping house in the evenings. We had sent away for a parcel of clothes suitable for a young businesswoman, and after a little work on them I was able to look sufficiently respectable to start on my new career.

Marshall Brothers was an old established firm of religious publishers in Paternoster Row which I fell in love with on sight. To get there it was a penny ride on a tram to Smithfield from Highbury Corner, and then a walk through the narrow street past St Bartholomew's Church and Hospital, across Newgate Street to the Row. To save money we always walked the whole journey in the morning, and rode back in the evening. I don't know if Paternoster Row was burnt down in the

Great Fire of London or whether these were the remains of mediaeval buildings — they certainly looked like it both outside and in, and I always had the feeling that if one pushed one's fingers fairly hard against the rotting wood and plaster they would go through, and one would be able to grasp a handful of crumbling stuff and powder it up.

Lots of the upper stories hung out over the pavements, and our premises had obviously at one time been a largish shop with storerooms behind and two storeys above. Now on the right was a counter from which the publications were sold — wholesale, of course — and on the left wall another one on which packing was done. A long narrow passage went through to the back, which was split up by wooden partitions. There was the secretary's office, so crowded you could hardly move, the accountant's office, the same size but it only had to house one person and all the ledgers, and several other dark dens full of shelves crammed with papers large and small which presumably the packing staff knew all about. Further back still were two perfectly ghastly WCs, and there was no cloakroom or place where we could make a cup of tea or anything.

The first floor was quite a respectable suite of offices where the three partners spent their days. There were two old gentlemen, Mr Edwin and Mr Herbert, who bumbled about gently and presumably performed some function. Red-faced and paunchy they poddled in gently at about 10.30 and left by 4 o'clock. Mr Fred, the nephew, worked hard all day, and worked the staff hard, too.

The top floor housed the Editorial offices where Mr Maclean, a meek, mild Scotsman, edited the main publication, *The Life of Faith*, a very paying proposition, and with the help of a delightful lady assistant named Miss Holyoake, who was a cousin or second cousin or something of a rising Australian politician, churned out about a dozen or more, each of which was the official publication of some charity or other. There was a constant coming and going through the shop and up the stairs of more or less seedy looking elderly clergymen, and I realised afterwards that our busy hive was really a collection box into which countless widows up and down the country sent their mites to be stored and then distributed to these elderly clergymen for the especial charities which they paid Marshall Brothers to advertise for them in one of their numerous publications.

The most exciting male member of the staff, who was hardly ever in so he didn't have an office, was Mr White, the Advertising Manager, a large, jolly, handsome young man, who was kept busy selling space in *The Life of Faith* and the multitudinous other bits and pieces we printed, and of course, he was the most important person there. The elderly clergymen might moan that their four inch double column appeal for neat cotton dresses for M'Bongo maidens had been crowded inside the back page and overpowered by "Gloves for Lepers" and little Mr McLeod might snap at the crowding of his leader page lay-out by pleas for orphans of Matabele tribal settlements, but the "mites" pouring in day after day in the postman's bag changed the fretting to smiles, and the elderly clergymen felt justified in their life work, and perhaps wondered if they might honestly give themselves another ten pounds this year on their salary. Marshall Brothers' bank account benefited considerably, though I am sure all the money donated did arrive at the intended destination, less a commission, of course.

I thought it pathetic, and rather wonderful, in those early days of war, how those old ladies whose incomes must have dropped almost to rock bottom, squeezed out their "mites" for their black brothers and sisters, and they sent such loving, encouraging letters to their especial elderly clergyman whose work they had followed for years. To a girl of seventeen, who knew what life was like here in England, it seemed absolutely idiotic, but I suppose it made the old gentlemen's lives seem worthwhile. Sometimes they had no money to spare, and would send along a piece of old fashioned jewellery which had "been in the family" for years, but the amount of money entered up in the ledger after its sale always seemed pitifully small. These things I saw when I had been with the firm for several months. At first I was Dorothy's assistant in her crowded office, which also housed the Editor's typist.

I started my first morning looking quite demure and neat in a navy blue dress with a white collar and ruffle at my throat, a new pair of shoes (4/11d at Roberts) and a feeling that the world was at my feet. I still had a great hero worship for Dorothy, and was bubbling over with joy at the thought of working with her but as we walked from the flat through Upper Street to

Smithfield, then past St Bartholomew's Hospital with its great iron gate and spreading lawns, across Newgate Street to Ivy Lane into Paternoster Row, I had my first insight into the position my sister expected me to occupy. She was having no rivals! I was to be obedient to her, speak when I was spoken to, avert my gaze and get on with my work if and when Mr Fred or anyone else important came in to the office, and generally be a hard-working little mouse. Christian name familiarity was not to be allowed. She, to me, was Miss Roberts, and I should be to her and everyone else, Miss G. This plonked my old inferiority complex right back in place again, and it was a long time before I managed to shake it off again.

She could not, however, find much fault with my work, and all the others seemed to like me quite well. Miss Bell, the Editor's typist, was a dear, a pretty, plump dark-haired Scottish girl with a mole on her chin with a considerable bunch of whisker sticking out of it. She had a delicious sense of humour and a lovely giggle, and we managed to have a bit of quiet fun together. She had a boy friend, though she was very respectful about him, and lived in a small town in Essex, I think it was Romford, where her father edited the local newspaper.

The three packing staff were most polite, and Grossmith the senior one, a great hulking dark fellow, used to appear to hold his breath when I had to speak to him, as though I were a piece of porcelain that might shatter if too much wind blew upon me. The head of the packing department was an elderly man, most

Godly and a Lay Preacher, a nasty, bad tempered hypocrite whose every second word to the young men was an oath when he was in a bad mood, but in a good mood almost worse, for he would mix texts with a kind of servile nagging which would reduce the young fourteen year olds to tears.

The other man we had, a most superior person in charge of sales, was unashamedly of German extraction, and made no secret of the fact that he had no real need to work as he had a private income. He enjoyed handling books, of which the shelves behind him were full, many of them of lovely soft leather, tooled and with gold lettering, all religious, yet he was a cheerful, confessed atheist. He was the only one there who did not kowtow to the Marshall brothers but met them on equal ground. The firm published and owned the copyright of Spurgeon's Sermons, which according to Mr Ebling, sold like hot cakes, and were the fount of the rivers of wisdom and goodness that flowed from the pulpits up and down the country every Sunday.

I worked with Doff for several months in that crowded office, and apart from plump little Miss Bell it was very dull indeed. All the equipment was so ancient. I had never seen a typewriter like the one allotted to me, it was called a "Yost" and was like a sort of bird's nest of rusty twigs with an inkpad forming the bottom, and there were three rows of lettered keys round the top. Somehow, when one hit the letters the twigs sorted themselves out, struck the inked pad, and came up again and stretched up and hit the paper which one had wound through the platen roll which seemed a yard away from the rest of the apparatus, and somehow a row of letters appeared and one was able to type a letter, but how I was never quite able to fathom. Perhaps I was an idiot, as Doff told me, I know I am not mechanically minded, but when she went away for a week later on I found her nice modern machine very easy and pleasant to use, and Mr Fred told her on her return that Miss G was very competent. Like Queen Victoria, she was not pleased.

Our internal telephone was one of those you blow down, and the outside telephone was like an old lady's ear trumpet hanging on a hook, and you talked to a cup on the wall, while the switchboard was like a large flat box with lots of pegs stuck in, each with a wire dangling and a number above it and a hole below, and you moved the numbered peg you wanted and wound a handle, and pushed the peg in the hole. Miss Bell and I said that our telephone equipment came from the Ark when the Dove had finished with it, but once again Dorothy was not amused. She made my life pretty miserable those first few months. She would give me wodges of things to type but the least interesting possible, with "Do this, Miss G.", "Do that, Miss G," never any conversation more than to a grubby, dirty-nosed little office boy, and in front of other people snubbed me unmercifully, but she got so that she didn't switch back when we left the office but went along as if I wasn't there, and I tagged along behind her feeling like a mongrel puppy with a can on its tail.

Other people were beginning to be nice to me as if I had at last become respectable and worthwhile, as I had so much longed to be, but not Doff. I think she always saw me as a scraggy, leggy charity child with my hair cut short, and didn't want anyone to think she was connected with me. And Edith had never been anything but a beast to me, so she treated me the same, even to the "Miss G", and as Mother had to sleep most of the daytime, she just fell in with them when she was around with us, and I spent my evenings and weekends doing the chores in a sort of fog of disapproval.

The job Doff always did was the shopping. I don't remember how much money I was getting at the office, but I handed it all over (it wasn't much) into the kitty, and was given five shillings back for my weekly expenses. Lunch at the JP cost sixpence, fourpence for beef pudding and mash, very good, or sausage and mash, and twopence for a currant pudding or apple pudding or some such, quite nice and filling. I could seldom spare a penny for a bus to Smithfield, but my cardboard-soled shoes always needed mending because of walking. Absolutely necessary personal things swallowed up the other two shillings and sixpence.

I used to gaze at and long for the chocolate and toffees in the sweet shops in Upper Street, but they were quite beyond my reach. Mother gave generously towards the household expenses, but Edith dodged the kitty whenever she could. Dorothy always ordered the groceries at the nice shop near Highbury Corner, she bought well and never haggled over prices, and they treated her as if she was a lady — as indeed she looked and sounded — and the goods were always delivered by teatime. The butcher was the same, and we always had

229

a lovely leg of lamb or piece of sirloin, we took in cake or bread, and I had never lived so well in my life as we did those weekends. The cold meat spread over a few suppers, and for the rest we bought as we came from work: kippers, herrings, smoked haddock, sausages all good and extraordinarily cheap.

We did not leave the office till six, but the shops all kept open later than now, and though we would arrive home famished — a twopenny pudding didn't last all that time — in a short time they were cooked and eaten, to be followed by slices and slices of bread and jam, and washed down by cups of hot tea. Is there much in the world better than the feeling of young hunger satisfied? No slimming like greyhounds. I did the cooking and washing up, and I don't think much else was done.

At the weekends Dorothy and I went to church, not a local one, but all the way to Westminster Chapel where the Rev. Campbell Morgan reigned. I say "reigned" purposely, for he certainly was the king there. Apparently each Sunday for several years Doff had spent the whole of her Sundays there, absorbing the atmosphere this wonderful man emitted. There seemed to be quite a fair-sized inner circle of worshippers. They would get there early to take morning Sunday School, then attend morning service. Dr Morgan was a wonderful preacher, and never spoke for less than forty minutes, then after the service they had dinner together. I suppose there was a rota of helpers, but as I wasn't there I cannot say. Then they took afternoon Sunday School, and some time or other had tea, then there was evening service, and fitted in somewhere was a Bible lecture.

Of course I know these inner church circles were fairly safe matrimonial agencies, where church members felt their young were safe to mix. I have seen them all my life, and very nice and sensible they were too, but Dorothy wasn't like that, more like a nun. She took life very, very seriously, and filled notebook after notebook with shorthand notes of sermons and lectures, and in all that time never had what is now called a "boyfriend", yet she was as pretty as a picture. But I didn't fit in very well. She didn't introduce me happily to her friends as her young sister, but when she had to mention me I was Miss Gee, as they took her to mean, and certainly not welcomed into her circle, but then I found her circle so boring. I liked girls my own age and boys a little older, but not too much, but certainly boys, and I soon had two or three nice and friendly and promising. I got so tired of her interminable nagging sermons on the way home in the little underground bus, I was nearly sick with fright in the darkness, and always felt I couldn't hold on any longer, just as it popped out of the black tunnel on to the Embankment, and somehow her grumbling voice made it worse. When we arrived home she would tell all my wickednesses to the others. It was always the same when I was a little girl, how I had been giggling with Wally Hacker in the Sermon, and how David Philpot had tried to walk to the bus with us and I had hung back with him instead of hurrying on with her and Miss Something or other, and Edith joining in, she who played high jinks with who knows who each weekend, and came home looking like a cat who has stolen the cream.

So I got fed up and said I couldn't afford the fare to Westminster — I certainly couldn't — and I was going to Union Chapel instead. So I was a wicked person once more, who couldn't appreciate all that was done for her. But I dug my heels in and went my own way. Union Chapel was just the other side of Upper Street and not far from the buildings where we lived, and I settled in straight away and everyone was very nice to me, and I was made to feel that I mattered, and that I was someone worth having. I was soon teaching in the Sunday School, and had my own coterie of small girls waiting for me outside the building and fighting to hold my hand and to sit next to me in the chapel when Sunday School was over.

There was one pretty little girl called Hilda, who became my shadow. Her family lived in a lovely house in Highbury Place, and her mother invited me to tea, and I became quite a friend of the family. There were only five of them, Mr and Mrs Brown and three children, of whom Hilda was the youngest, and the house had about twelve rooms. Mr B really carried on his business of a medical supplier's there, in the big rooms in the basement, but unfortunately since the war had started there was no business, or precious little, and with my memories of pinching and penury I imagined that things were going very badly for them and Mrs B would say with a sigh that the house was much too big for them, and there was far too much work for her to do alone. I began to scheme and plan and hope in my mind.

I had an idea that often her remarks were directed at me, and that she was trying to tell me that they wished to let a flat to us, but I was still too diffident to believe that such good fortune could be mine, to live in a charming house with hot water and a bathroom and such nice people, so I hung back and said nothing for the time being. We could quite easily afford to pay for it, I thought, and the Browns had met Doff and loved her, but they had not seen Mother, and if I even mentioned them to her she would toss her head and sniff, and say things about my fine friends, and find me jobs so that I hadn't time to visit them.

Furniture was a terrible stumbling block. I tried to imagine our four wooden chairs and deal table in the lovely drawing room — it had three long windows down to the ground, and a lovely curved recess each side of the fireplace, and with the Browns' furniture was gracious and charming. I decided to do what I think women have done from time immemorial when they want something those in authority don't want, talk about it openly, making it clear that it was much too good for the likes of us, that the Browns would want more genteel people than we were, getting them interested and then woodenly refusing to discuss it.

I stalled like this for weeks. It was December when we went to the Buildings, and till March we just froze and had no comfort at home at all, but it prepared the ground. I think it was January that first year we had the terrible freezing fog. People talk about "smog" now, but they don't know what a real yellow pea-souper was like. Neither did I till then. Of course every house was warmed by open coal fires, most of them in several rooms unless the people were very poor, and there was no such thing as "smokeless fuel". On every roof rows of chimneys belched out clouds of smoke, and in so many streets these were broken by factory chimneys doing the same thing, only more so. Most of the local railway stations which are now electric underground had their own steam trains, which puffed happily by the platforms, while black gnomes shovelled coal into the engine and you walked along and groped for the door handles in stygian darkness, and looked in horror at the soot you had accumulated, once you were in the carriage.

For days and days that January the air we breathed was just thick yellow sulphur-laden smoke in the daytime, black ditto by mid-afternoon. What made it worse — though very exciting — was that because of the inadequacy of the street lighting great fires were lit on each corner of the footpath at every road junction, each one in charge of a man whose job it was to keep it stirred up with a very long rod — it had to be long because of the length of the flames and the intense heat — and of course its brilliance had the effect of making the surrounding darkness look more intense, and the soot and smoke each fire threw up poisoned the atmosphere for a considerable distance. I remember leaning up against a wall watching a man stirring up a fire and thinking it must be just like Hades with Satan stirring up the flames, the man with his long rod

234

silhouetted against the leaping tongues, his long tattered coat, to my imagination like a long forked tail, and everything else also black darkness. And the cries of the very few men who with lanterns were trying to guide their horses and vans back to their yards, suggested the souls in torment.

Westminster Chapel had a Social Club, though I had not seen anything of it on the occasions I had been with Doff, and a very popular feature of it was the Rambling Club. One Saturday, March 6th, to be precise, they were visiting the printing works and offices of the *News of The World*, a conducted tour, and for some reason or other I was told I was going; perhaps they were short on numbers or something. We were shown all sorts of interesting things, but after all these years I have nothing but a confused impression of heat and the smell of ink and oil and the noise of machinery. To swell the numbers, the secretary of the club had brought along a colleague of his, a Civil Servant, in appearance a most correct, conventional young man. I found afterwards he was not yet nineteen. He wore a suit, the darkest of dark grey, black socks with red clocks and black shoes, and a grey tie. In one hand he carried a neatly rolled umbrella, and in the other a bowler hat, and his hair looked lacquered, so neatly was it plastered down on his head with oil. And glory be, he was quite six feet tall. As neither of us knew many of the rest of the party, perhaps it was not surprising that we soon found ourselves walking together. And as he appeared to understand quite a bit of what the man in front was telling us, which was more than I did, I found myself enjoying the tour immensely. The pièce de resistance was each of us having our names set up in type and presented to us, but the typesetter turned all roguish, and presented me with a piece of metal with both our names, side by side. We all went back to the Chapel Hall where there was tea and a social evening was planned, but Duncan White and I sat and talked until it was time to go home.

There were some decorous indoor games, I remember, like passing the ring round on a piece of string, and unpacking the parcel, played at church socials from time immemorial, but behind the backs of well-behaved Dorothy and her middle-aged lady friends who were keeping the circle as all well-behaved church socialites should, there were several pairs of young people getting to know each other, their likes and dislikes, their hobbies, their work and their play. How marvellous it was to find how much we had in common. We loved the same authors and books, music was the same joy to each of us, we loved long walks alone, and incidentally we were both lonely young folk with no friends and no money to spend on anything but walking.

We found we had lived within a few miles of each other for about four years, and that seemed magical. While I had wandered round Hull streets, and scrambled by the warehouses and along the wharves by the river, climbing up on the top of the pier and gazing across to Immingham, which he said was a sort of dock suburb of Grimsby, he had been staying on and off with his great-aunt, whose husband had been on the Town

236

Council, and had served his term as Mayor. My heart went into my boots, and I started explaining that my family weren't anything like that, and he said I looked and sounded wonderful to him, and seemed to know more than all his aunts put together.

At some extra noisy period of the games we slipped away into another room, and in the comparative quiet continued our exploration of each other's minds, and likes and dislikes, and for the first time the difference between the male and female outlook on life came home to me. I was enthusing about the little animals and birds at Weston, and he said how his father loved birds, and how he had an albino blackbird he had shot and had had stuffed, and how he had quite a notable collection of stuffed birds which were rare to their neighbourhood. He was quite enthusiastic as he told me how they had got up early on Sunday mornings and gone down with their guns to the sand hills, taking their spaniel dog Bess and she would "put up" rabbits from the scrub, and they would let them run a distance on the grassy loose sand, and then each in turn shooting at one, and how of course, you had to get them in one shot if you could. And the birds would rise from the low bushes at the gunfire, and so of course, you shot them for the fun of the thing. Not the white blackbird. He had sung each evening for a week from the plum tree in the garden, and his father had studied it through his glasses to see what it was, and then shot it when he found it was a freak.

Although I knew this side of country life quite well, I could never get reconciled to it, and must have looked

237

my disapproval, and I remember I said, "And then I suppose you went to Church," for he had told me his father was a lay preacher and they went to church morning and evening. And his face really did fall, as people say, and he was puzzled at my disapproval, and explained gently that of course in the countryside you shot "for the pot" — that was the rabbits. "And the little birds?" I said, and he went red and hesitated, and said, "You practice your shooting. It's one thing shooting at a fixed target, but quite another thing shooting on the wing,", and then, thoughtfully, "I've never thought about it before, but I'll never shoot a small bird for fun again, only bigger ones, like duck, for the pot."

Doff had been trying to catch my eye for some time before we changed rooms, and now came in more than a little cross, and said we were late, and started saying "Goodnight" charmingly to Duncan, and I willed him as hard as I could not to slink away, and he swallowed very hard and said as he lived not far away from us, could he not escort us home? He was quite clever and artful, and talked to Doff more than to me in the bus, and I sat quiet. He came all the way to our horrible buildings, and didn't faint when he saw them and said "Goodnight" to Doff like a courteous old gentleman, but behind her retreating back he whispered, "City Temple, tomorrow, please. I will be here at half past five." I tumbled up the concrete stairs as fast as I could, but by the time I got in the flat door they had heard of my dreadful behaviour, and the storm broke. I was utterly shameless, and had disgraced Dorothy by

238

talking to a strange young man all the evening, and everybody had noticed. "You bet they had," I said, "and most of them would have given their eyebrows to have had him themselves. And what's more, he's calling for me tomorrow evening and we are going to the City Temple." And on that exit line I scooted into the next room and soon tumbled into bed. I pretended to be asleep when Mother came in, but for hours lay scheming, and looking for a plan to make them agree to leave those awful buildings and go to the Browns' flat.

Morning brought no solution, and I hurried round getting breakfast, doing the chores and preparing the dinner so that I could go to my church. Of course I was still in disgrace, but Mother was still in bed, she "lay in" on Sunday, and when I was ready to go, to my great astonishment both Doff and Edith came with me. My faithful Hilda was waiting for me, and we all sat with the Browns, and after service even Edith was friendly towards them, so they had met all three of us; only Mother remained, but of course, she was a very big hurdle for conventional people to climb, unless she wanted to make an impression, when she could be as nice as anything.

I managed to get tea finished and cleared away early, and tidied myself ready for my first date — I hadn't to change clothes or anything, as the navy blue costume and largish straw hat I had worn on the Saturday and to church in the morning were my "best things", the only ones I had. I was scared stiff they would say I was not to go, but to my great surprise Doff came out of the flat and down the stone stairs with me. I blurted out,

"Oh, are you going to Westminster Chapel?" and she said, "No, I'm coming with you and this young man," just like a maiden aunt of fifty, I thought. However, there was Duncan waiting outside on the pavement, rolled umbrella and bowler hat and all, and Doff was charming to him. I was in disgrace, but he wasn't. I thought, knowing them, that she had come prepared to "choke him off", but I don't think she knew how.

He had brought an envelope full of photographs of his father and his aunt and innumerable uncles, and their house and the farm at Willoughby where the uncles and his grandmother lived, and his father's trap and the pony called Bob, and one of a tall thin lady, quite elegant, and an equally tall thin gentleman, with a top hat and a chain and an ornament round his neck. "Great Auntie and Great Uncle Ashlyn Grant," he said, "the Mayor and Mayoress of Grimsby," and tried to sound very pompous and important, but as fortunately he was not pompous at all, but only an overgrown schoolboy trying to make an impression, he straight away laughed at himself and said, "As a matter of fact they are not because Uncle Ashlyn has been dead for ten years at least, but this was him once." He had to do most of his talking to Doff, for my heart sank lower and lower into my boots. I could not imagine his aunt, who lived with them and who had a hard, hard face with sticky-out teeth, being at all pleasant to me, and all the people I had known who had pleasant houses and farms like this had looked on me as a most reprehensible ragamuffin when I was younger. Yes, his aunt was rather like the elder Miss Yates at Hull. Oh, dear!

Then all of a sudden he jumped up, said, "Goodbye, Miss Roberts, have a good service. This is our stop." He took my arm and jumped me off the bus, leaving Doff high and dry as the bus jerked off again. We walked along Kingsway decorously, without speaking, till we reached the Hall, then stopped and looked at each other and started to laugh, tentatively at first, for we were still comparative strangers, then more freely, and I remember a sort of melting, comfortable feeling spreading inside that this person, male, and better placed than myself, was a friend, whose reactions I could share, and who could share mine. He grinned all over his pleasant, rather ugly face and said, "I think we did that rather well, don't you?" And we went into church.

The organist, I think, was Frank Idol. I had never heard organ-playing, as such, before, only once at Hull as the accompaniment to Stainer's *Crucifixion* when it sounded melodious and charming, but this I thought awful. He played Bach's *Toccata and Fugue*, and it was just noise. It didn't try to tell me anything, but just blared and roared round and round the hall. I thought at the time how ignorant and awful I was to dare to criticise in my mind organ-playing under these conditions, and by a well-known organist, but it was no good. I just couldn't bear it, and to me organ-playing was anathema until quite twenty-five years later, when my son, a student at the Guildhall, had brought one of his professors home to tea — he taught composition

241

and organ and I more or less apologised because I detested organs. "No," he said, "It isn't organs you detest, it's organists. The average English organist isn't happy unless he has all the stops out, the lot, and just lets rip." And he said how a new French school of organists were coming up, and how delicate and charming their playing was, and thank goodness I have heard them for myself since. How wonderfully fortunate we are now, for so many years a person without money just could not hear real music unless he or she lived in the heart of London or some other large city, but now I, an old, infirm woman, need only turn a knob, and the Third Programme will pour out chamber music, orchestral or vocal music, opera — all of the finest and best. But I digress.

I had to let Duncan see me to the entrance of our gloomy Buildings, and we were still standing talking when Doff came home and went up the stairs without comment, except to tell me not to be long. We arranged to go to Union Chapel the next Sunday, and I ran up to the flat. They were all pretty glum, probably because no one had got the supper ready with me being out, and Doff sniffed and said she would have thought Mr White would have something better to do than to stand with me down in that horrible entrance. Like Brer Rabbit I said nuffin', but thought a lot.

Next Sunday we went to Union together both morning and evening, and young Hilda Brown was thrilled to bits and hung on his arm, and whispered to me, "Oh she did LOVE my young man." I said, "Sshh, he was only a friend," and she giggled and said, "Oh,

242

he's nice." Everyone at Union seemed to share her opinion, and I think my stock went up a lot. Anyhow, unless we had planned some treat or other, we went to Union together twice every Sunday, and for the first time in my life I was the target of shooting envious glances from the many smart daughters of the well-padded gentlemen who were the pillars of the Church. It was early 1915, and tall, respectable, well-dressed young men were thin on the ground. There were the Benson girls, Leisa, Gladys and Madge, whose father kept the leather shop in Upper Street, and the Broughs, whose father was something big in the City and an Alderman, and Rose Elsom, and oh, dozens more, and they none of them had to go to "business" as they called it, but "helped" at home, and they were all aching to have young men, and there were no "eligible" ones at church to be had. There were two elderly bachelor brothers, I remember, named Hazell, between fifty and sixty I should think. They were very busy in the Church, one played the harmonium in the Sunday School, and the other was in charge of the school, and they had a wonderful time. They were really very fond of young women, but probably had been rather shy in their youth, but now they were really making up for it. All very circumspect, no doubt, but they were always surrounded by tribes of "girls" from about twenty-five to sixty, and they — Bertie and Ben Hazell — used to giggle and simper, and the "girls" used to bring them flowers.

Around that time the D'Oyley Carte company came to the Marlborough Theatre, and we saw most of the

Gilbert and Sullivan Operas, and I always associated the Hazells and their following of "young" ladies with *Patience*, and Duncan and I thought it would be funny to place a lily on the harmonium, but we couldn't find one, and anyhow, we decided, no-one would see the point. Curiously enough, it never occurred to me that I might lose Duncan to one of these girls, and I think perhaps because he was so used to the "chapel" atmosphere, and also because he was a really nice and unassuming person, he just fitted in with us, and was pleasant and friendly to everyone else. The important gentlemen shook his hand morning and evening, and were soon calling him by his Christian name, and soon "our" special seat was kept for us in the gallery, front row.

I think Easter must have come in April that year, and we had our first outing together. Both he and I had very little money to spend, but we found we both loved walking and the countryside was very much nearer to Highbury than it is now. I can remember it as if it were yesterday. We took a tram and went on top to the top of Highgate Hill, and I was scared stiff that the whole contraption would slide down the hill backwards. My knees nearly buckled with fright as I tumbled off the step of the tram, but in a most manly way he held me up, and as we started to stride out, a wonderful smell assailed our nostrils. On the left hand side of the path was an, even for then, old-fashioned eating house, and someone had just opened the door, and the smell of good roast beef which came across to us just could not be ignored. It was about twelve o'clock, and a cold,

244

misty, foggy morning, and I had done quite a bit of housework, and he had walked quite a way from his "digs" round to fetch me, and in the heady, holiday state we were in good sense — pounds, shillings and pence just didn't count, and we were through that door and inside before you could say "knife". It seemed very dark at first, but then through the swirls of tobacco smoke the glow of the red lamps on each of the tables began to look very cosy. The seats were not chairs, but dark wooden highback settles with straight backs like boxes. The tables matched and had clean white cloths on, and we had roast beef and Yorkshire pudding, baked potatoes and cabbage — man-sized helpings — and baked jam roly-poly, and I leaned back against my hard settle, full to the top and wondered hazily how I could offer my one and only shilling to Duncan to help pay — for even I knew that gentlemen always pay for ladies. Then I surfaced to find he was paying the bill and looking very cheerful; it was one shilling each! How can one possibly compare wages then and now when the charges are so different?

The sun was struggling through and it was warmer when we went out, or was it our full stomachs that made it seem so? We strode out and were soon crossing fields and walking down Summers' Lane, down Friern Barnet Lane through the water splash and past the authentic well where Queen Elizabeth drank in 1560 something, and through to the pretty ancient town of Barnet, and the countryside beyond. In 1915, so much of what is now a sprawling suburb was open countryside.

At about four o'clock, as we were getting hungry again we saw a clean little terrace cottage with a notice — TEAS — in the window. The door was open, and the way led straight into a little room with pink geraniums in the window, and a round table with a lace-edged cloth in the centre, and a bell which said "Ring". We picked it up and rang, and a nice plump old lady popped in and said "The kettle's just boiling, sit right down and rest your feet while I make the tea," so we did just that, while she bustled in with a laden tray, and in next to no time the table was set with brown and white bread and butter and home-made plum jam in a pretty pot with a lid on and a cat as the knob and a hole for the spoon, and buttered scones and a home-made sponge cake, and a fat tea pot steaming at the spout, and hot water and lots of milk and sugar. Then two pretty flowery cups and saucers and plates from half a dozen that were set out waiting on a side table, and she left us, as she said, to get on with it. And we did! Nearly all the bread and butter went, and the scones, though we did restrain ourselves and only have one piece of cake each. She had cut such big slices one couldn't possibly give way and have two. There'd have been no cake left. When she came back she said that would be 1/- each, and was that satisfactory!

She asked if we would we like to go in the garden. There were crocuses and daffodils, and something that attracted me even more. An obvious Privy was down at the end, and after all that tea I was dying to use it, but I could not bring myself to go there, and I was pretty certain Duncan was in the same boat, but we were both abnormally shy about such things. He had no sisters, I had no brothers, and we had no experience to fall back on. Now, a girl who has no qualms on the subject — "Just a minute, going to the loo" or "Going to the Ladies" — how much easier life is for them. We set off along the narrow tree-lined lane, and I looked longingly at the small copses on either hand, wishing I could get lost in one for a few moments and Duncan seemed to have gone all miserable when all of a sudden he said, "Excuse me a minute," and slipped across the little dry ditch and disappeared, to amble back a little higher up, looking supremely pleased with himself.

He started looking at his watch, and said it was getting late, and we might find it difficult to get on a bus, and then I felt worse and thought, "Oh, dear, he is bored with me and won't want to have a day out again." Instead of the short cut to Hadley Highstone he had been talking about, he said that if we were in the queue by seven o'clock we wouldn't have any trouble getting home. By the time we did reach the pub where we had to queue for the bus I was very quiet, and he decided I was overtired and blamed himself a lot, but once we were in the yard of the pub and I saw two women walking towards a door marked "Ladies", it was all I could do to restrain myself and walk decorously towards them. I too felt a lot better after that, and we amused ourselves till the bus came half an hour later, watching the fat, grunting, squealing pigs up to their stomachs in the mud, and the hens and some ducklings who were driving a scruffy little hen foster mother nearly frantic by flapping about in all the puddles they could find. That half hour's wait for the bus was sheer heaven. The queue kept growing, but the two women were very kind and kept our places for us while we rooted round that pub yard and the paddock and the stables adjoining it like a pair of silly children.

We had had a heavenly day, with lots of good for it had been so cheap there was no worry attached to it. I was tired out, of course, and sat on the back seat of the bus by the window, and there was a rosy glow over everyone, and as it gradually grew darker Duncan's arm slipped behind my back and my head slid just that little bit onto his shoulder and I stayed in that half way state between sleeping and waking, when every good noise is magnified and everything bad is dulled, and one just knows that one is safe and happy.

It must have been about nine o'clock when we reached the Buildings, and tired as I was I didn't go straight up the stairs. I just didn't want this wonderful day to end, and Duncan certainly made no move to go, so we just stood hidden in the dark entrance, doing nothing, close together, oh, for quite a while, then, all of a sudden, Duncan pushed his arm round my shoulders, pulled me towards him and KISSED me, or at least, presumably tried to, but he only succeeded in hitting his nose, which was fairly large, on my ear. I felt myself go hot all over, and said, in a silly little voice, "Oh, you shouldn't have done that!" To which he replied, "No, I didn't mean to that time, but I do this," and he grabbed me again, and planted a very firm but chaste salute on my cheek. How very tame this would seem to modern young people, but to us, we were in

248

heaven. Bells of joy were ringing, and the stars had all come out and were simply blazing down. Just one mild kiss between two young people who had spent a wholesome, happy day together, and the world was changed. We clung onto each other's hands for a minute or two, and it was as if a pledge had passed between us — as indeed it had, silently, and then I disengaged mine, whispered "Goodnight" and turned and started up the stairs. Duncan walked with me across the cold stone hall to where the little gaslight burned in a wire cage, then held my hand against his cheek for a moment, and stood there while I went up.

The others were not in, fortunately, or they would certainly have wanted to know why I was sitting around "mooning", but I presume I set some food out, ate my own, and made the bed. Poor Mother, I did so hate sleeping with her, and this arrangement of permanent night duty pleased me very much, because I had the bed to myself. She was so slovenly in her ways, and never attempted to make or air the bed when she left it, so one of the first things I did when she had left was to pull the sheets and blankets right down over the foot of the bed, and roll back the flock mattress, so that the air could percolate through the straw palliasse.

That night I waited for the bed to air and thought over our lovely day and Doff came in, very late. She had a friend whose husband was a Captain in the Army and away at the Front, and Doff had started spending most evenings with her. She was very unhappy and complaining, and I felt she made most unreasonable demands on Doff, who used to come in very late and in very poor spirits — not to say downright bad-tempered. I had to listen to all poor Emily's woes until Doff had got them off her chest, and then, of course, I had to be told all I ought to be doing for tomorrow morning, for our precious Easter holiday was over. Though I had determined to try to tell her what a lovely day I had had, and what a wonderful friend Duncan was, she just wasn't interested. Or so I thought, but during the week the subject of the Browns kept coming up. From Mother, "What do they want to let part of their house for?" From Doff, "Oh well, it takes too much keeping up." I realised Doff was as keen on the idea as I was, and also knew the best way to handle Mother, so I came in as a sort of chorus, with, "Oh well, we couldn't possibly afford to live there," to be snapped up at last with what did I know about it, "We could probably afford it better than a lot of other people."

This went on in a desultory sort of way for several days, till I discovered Mother was really fighting against an invitation from Mrs Brown to go to tea on Saturday afternoon. I hadn't been told about it but I discouraged it all I could, till wild horses wouldn't have kept Mother away though she wouldn't give a straight answer as to whether she would go or not. I chanced it, and told Hilda at the Camp Fire Girls meeting (Yes, we had Camp Fire Girls because the Minister thought Girl Guides, with their outdoor uniforms, were not ladylike, and I was one of the officers) that Doff, Mother and I would be coming to tea. I polished up a pair of patent-toed, button boots which Mother didn't wear much because they pinched, and brushed up a rather

250

pretty black fur toque with a feather in it which she didn't wear because Jessie had sent it to her a year or two before, the last time Doff left home; I think it was a sort of peace offering. I thought with them and the winter coat she was still wearing — a sort of imitation ponyskin, black and shiny, she would look quite nice, if she wanted to. I left the clothes casually in the front of the cupboard so they would be the first to hand and I didn't want her to feel rushed, we'd have to get her up earlier than normal on a Saturday, and give her something light and tempting for dinner without her noticing that we were trying to keep her in a good mood. I screwed up my courage to talk to Doff about it on the way home from the office and to my astonishment found that she was determined to move, and had been working on Mother for weeks. I asked why on earth she hadn't talked to me about it, and she looked down her nose at me and more or less reminded me that I was "Miss G", the young person who did the chores, and she was the person who made the decisions. I boiled with resentment inside, but years of being squashed had left me unable to lose my temper, so we did our shopping, and carried on with our normal Saturday afternoon arrangements.

I made some tea when it was time for Mother to get up, and Doff carried a cup in to her, and sat and talked to her while she drank it, and that was enough to put her in a really good mood. She loved Dorothy so very deeply, her feeling for her was totally different from anything she felt for we others. Edith and Jessie just didn't care for her at all — it would have been surprising if they did — but when I was little I hung on to her for love, but she would push me away and say "Cupboard Love." Doff was her darling. Anyhow at four o'clock we three, with Mother looking quite respectable, though wispy as to hair, and very stiff-backed and on her dignity, went up the steps and rang-pulled the Browns' doorbell.

Those houses in Canonbury really are beautiful. I thought so nearly sixty years ago and thought so when I drove past in a mini-cab a week ago. A curved iron handrail ending in a sort of coil is on each side of the steps, and this house, our house, still had its original handsome fanlight over the door, and a solid, wrought-iron foot scraper by the steps. The hall was lofty, and, for a terrace townhouse, quite wide. The stairs were wide and handsome, with a beautiful carved, curving banister and newel post, and a charming decorated arch went across from one wall to the other, under part of which a long passage continued to the back of the house, the kitchen quarters, which were about half the width of the house. There were twelve rooms altogether, on four floors. A beautiful long room from front to back, with gorgeous windows to floor level, on the right of the hall, was used as the business premises, the front part was the packing room, and part of the back was Mr Brown's office, with a glass partition shutting off a strip as a laboratory where they did mysterious things with pestles and mortars, which eventually ended up at the packing end. There was not much sign of business in the first few months I saw the place, except I remember huge rolls of gauze which miraculously ended up as smallish blue wrapped bandages. I think Mr and Mrs Brown used to sit up nearly all night at first, doing things on little hand machines, like these bandages and rolls of lint and cotton wool, anything in their line that would keep a little of their trade going, and bring in a little money. Apparently at the beginning of the war certain commodities in which they had specialised, but which were imported, were no longer obtainable, and they had no trade to speak of.

The first handsome flight of stairs went straight up to a square landing, off which a door opened into a delicious medium-sized room, which must have been used as a nursery in the days of "nannies". There was still a brass-topped guard around the fireplace, and a low high-backed chair pushed back. A deepish recess on the right was curtained off, and behind the curtain the wall was set with brown and white picture tiles, with windmills — very Dutch looking — and there was a window in the centre of the wall, the panes covered with opaque paper with yellow ships. Set in the recess was a bath almost large enough for a whole family at once, framed in mahogany, and with a wide flat mahogany margin all round. This was to be our kitchen and bathroom! Leading off was another medium-sized room. These two rooms must have been over the large kitchen downstairs, and there were nice big cupboards too. A landing leading back to the front of the house led into a long drawing room, beautifully furnished in a Victorian way, with three long windows down to the floor, and curved recesses each side of the large fireplace, such a lovely shape with shelves, to show off china.

Off the landing on the left, before the big drawing room, was another good-sized room, and there Mrs Brown had set tea, and there she and Mother and Dorothy discussed what had seemed so difficult and impossible, and made it all seem easy. Apparently most of the details had already been fixed. The nursery-cum-bathroom was to be our kitchen, it had lino on the floor and cupboards, and our deal table and four wooden chairs would be just about adequate. The room that adjoined would be Doff's bedroom with her bed and chair, and I think she had a chest of drawers by then. The beautiful long front drawing room was to be ours, and I needn't have worried about the furniture, Mother was buying it all, just as it stood, at a proper valuation figure, and was going to pay so much a week, agreeing to pay it all within a year. Poor Mother, how she sat and preened herself. Apparently this job at the Arsenal was a very important and well-paid one, and for the first time in her life she could "call the tune" and lord it over little ladies like Mrs Brown who had hitherto had it easy, and oh dear, didn't she show it. Then we were to have two nice large attic bedrooms away at the top, one for Mother, where she could sleep undisturbed all day, and one for Edith and me to share. Our room had windows set inside a sort of parapet, one on each side of the room, and it was lovely to open the window at the bottom and lean out with one's arms across the wide stone sill outside, and see over the grey roofs and roads full of traffic to Hampstead Heath and Highgate,

254

miles of green grass and great trees — Highgate Hill first, mounting up and up, and then what looked like a succession of villages clustering along the Great North Road on to miles of countryside. I always thought of Dick Whittington and John Gilpin when I hung out across those slates.

The matter of the furniture and the money having been settled, Mother had to go, because most weekends she had to work, and I thought she looked tired. Probably her boots were pinching, or perhaps it was the thought of all the money she would have to pay out. But no, she said to Doff as they went down the wide stairs, "Are you pleased, Lovey, now you've got a nice home?" If Doff was pleased, it was worth anything. Mother loved that furniture. I don't suppose she dusted or polished it ever, but she kept it till she died, crusted with dirt in her later days, except one inlaid china cabinet, a real period piece, which had been high on the valuer's list, which she gave to Dorothy as a wedding present.

There was always a wall between Mother and Mrs Brown, and Doff didn't mix with them much. Edith, of course, was a shocker. She was a handsome, buxom young woman, a lazy slattern in the house which she seldom honoured with her presence, just in to meals and out again, and so far as work and money was concerned was most unreliable. She changed her jobs frequently, or rather, her employers changed her, and so she didn't bother about little things like handing over her share of the housekeeping money. When she did have money she would go down the West End most evenings and weekends, having what she called a good time, but she didn't talk much to us about it. One Sunday she did bring home two young French men she had met, they said they were art students. One was the nephew of quite a well-known artist. They were quite pleasant and we sat and drew with pencils and charcoal, and they seemed firmly to believe that if one could wield these materials with any degree of skill, one had no right to be doing anything else. I said, "What about earning money?" But they snapped their fingers and said, "Money, pffff!" I noticed they tucked into a pretty good tea. But I settled down with the Browns like one of the family, and they were always so sweet to me. I had always loved "keeping house" and I polished the furniture and lino till I could see my face in them, and of course there were meals to get too. The next year or so was the happiest I had ever had. I had Duncan, and we loved each other, but we were too young (or was it too inhibited) for it to worry us yet. That came later. We went out one night a week, just walking, and he came back home to supper, and of course we spent the weekends together, mostly at church. He loved our new rooms, and of course it was a long time before he realised the furniture was new to us as well, but the Browns welcomed him as much as they did me. For quite a while I had to spend most of my spare time doing housework, and used to get rather tired, but one day right out of the blue Mother found a "char", and she came every morning while we all stayed together. She washed up and kept our rooms and furniture clean, and I only had to do the cooking.

Poor Dorothy at this time was quite tied up with her friend Emily. She used to come in from the office, wash and have a meal, and go to Emily's, and they would sit and talk half the night, and I never knew quite what time Doff got home, but she used to look dreadfully tired out the next morning. Later on it got worse, for Emily decided she couldn't stay in her flat alone with her husband at the Front, so after a meal Doff would go round to her and stay all night, but Emily was too tired — or selfish — to give her breakfast in the morning, but would stay in bed asleep while poor old Doff walked round home for her breakfast, and then we walked to the office. Emily got up about twelve.

We, Duncan and I, had a nice little crowd of friends now, mostly from church, and we started a tennis club. About eight of us used to meet at the tennis courts in The Fields at 6.30 a.m. and play for an hour before breakfast — it must have been a dry summer! I had never even held a tennis racquet before, but I began to make a show quite quickly. I was so anxious not to look foolish and let Duncan down. He, of course, was fairly good, because some of his friends at home had tennis courts. No, he hadn't played at school. It was one of those things that "was not done" at boys' schools when we were young. Rugger, yes, and cricket, and boating, if you had a river near, as they had, but tennis, No! That was a girls' game. We played in the evenings, too, occasionally, but preferred the morning, when we had The Fields entirely to ourselves. I have an idea we got away without paying, too, as the man in charge of the courts was never there so early. I used to find it a little hard not to oversleep, but fortunately Mother had to go out very early, and because of Dorothy coming in early, she used to leave the door on the latch, and once or twice when I was not up ready for Duncan, he crept up the stairs and scratched softly on the door of our attic flight. Edith never stirred, she was a heavy sleeper, but I was a very light one and would tumble out of bed at the slightest sound, grabbing my clothes which were on a chair by my bed, scrambling into them as far away from Edith as I could get — drawers, camisole, petticoat, black stockings and a cotton frock and a pair of plimsolls.

Once and only once did things go wrong, but we were such a pair of innocents that nothing really went wrong, if you get my meaning. I heard the scratch on the door, flung the bedclothes back and my nightdress off in one movement, and then saw that Duncan was standing inside the door, staring at me, I dared not make a noise, but made a gesture with my hand for him to go away, but he said, all imploringly, "No, just one minute, just one little minute." and was kneeling by my bed. Gently he held my shoulders and pressed my head back on the pillow, and then leaned back on his heels and just looked — and I had not a scrap of covering on me. I really felt myself blush from my head to my feet, but he stammered out, "No, no, you are so beautiful, so very beautiful, and you are all mine." He leaned down and pressed his lips on my naked middle, hesitated just a bit, and then got up and went out and down the stairs very quietly.

258

I was completely bemused, for I had the vaguest idea of sex. I knew that terrible things happened to girls if they weren't careful with men, but what, I didn't know, though I knew from Weston and from reading, that if you weren't "careful" you ended up with a baby, but what physical contact produced the baby, and how or where was a sealed book. I remember once at Weston, telling Mrs Saville that I was worried because I knew nothing about how babies came. I remember I was sitting on the stone steps of the dairy, and she was churning. I had asked Evaline the previous day — it was about the time the Plumtree girl got into trouble — and she just grinned at me and said "Best way they can, head first," which of course, didn't help at all. Mrs Saville stopped churning and turned to me, her face red with effort, and brushed the wisps of hair back from her forehead with her hand. "Nay, Grace," she said, "One day when you've met your man and he's a good one, and you're near your wedding, you'll find it'll come easy to talk about these things. Only a little, just enough not to bed all ignorant." That was a great deal for her to say, and thank God it fell out as she said.

That episode, though we never referred to it, did make a difference to us. We were shy and gauche for a day or two, but when that passed off we did not easily fall back into the easy camaraderie which had been normal with us. Now, in the evenings, if we were alone in the drawing room, I was afraid of silences, and would keep on trying to "do" something, and if we touched accidentally I would draw away and I noticed his goodnight kisses were real kisses, very different from his earlier pecks.

It was summertime, fortunately, and we could go for walks, or go to The Fields and knock up for a bit with our racquets if there wasn't our own crowd or a spare court, and on the whole it worried us very little. I have been thinking about that tennis equipment. I couldn't have bought balls and a racquet, not yet. I think they must have been the leavings of an old tennis club at church, and we took it over. I think that September, Mother, Doff and Dith clubbed together and gave me a new tennis racquet as a birthday present. It wasn't a posh Slazenger or anything like that, but it was nice and springy, and light, with a slim grip, and a "Fish Tail" handle, and I thought I was the cat's whiskers, swishing it about. It probably cost all of 10/6d, and was still fairly firm when my daughter was thirteen.

I really was well started now on the road that I had sought for so long. I was eighteen, I spoke well, and was accepted by everyone who mattered as a well-brought up, well-educated young lady. I lived in a charming house in a good road — I need never shrink back out of sight so that people did not see what house I went into. I still bought most of my clothes through *Exchange and Mart*, but I had developed taste and neatness, and could alter them so that I looked fairly well dressed, besides which one could buy dress materials so very cheaply — 4d a yard at sale time if one searched, and though my stitches would not pass muster if examined closely, I could cut out well, and make quite smart-looking things from those precious 4d and 6d Weldon's patterns. It was difficult still to keep one's feet neat and smart looking, good shoes and stockings were still out of my reach. I was very fortunate in that since institution days I had been pretty. My hair was a bright reddish gold, not just fair, and my eyes brown, and my skin, which had been pale during my early teens when I had to work so hard, was now rosy and glowing. And I never had spots, a source of great satisfaction to me! Added to which I was tall but not too tall, and slim but not scraggy. And of course, I had Duncan, and I needed no-one else. He was my present and my future. So I was pretty well accepted as a "Young Lady", the goal which I had longed for, but had seemed so utterly impossible in those years of my childhood, after leaving the institution.

Now another step upwards came, quite unexpectedly. At the office Dorothy took great care that as "Miss G" I was very much under her thumb. I did the office boy jobs, the filing, and worked the ancient switchboard — which was the nearest I ever got with conversations with any of the "bosses", and on my old "Yost" I did reams of lists and whole volumes of copy typing, and every month I typed accounts and all the bits and pieces necessary for the young pince-nezed accountant next door. Apparently Mr Fred had formed a good opinion of my intelligence when I took Doff's place when she was away, and one day I was called into the Accounts Office, and there sat Mr Fred and fat Mr Edwin and the young Accountant. I was asked in the most pontifical way if I knew anything about figures and I said I had kept a set of books in my previous job in Hull — a cashbook and an Insurance Payments book, and had done bookkeeping in my commercial course at school. Mr Fred opened the ledger which was on the desk and asked if I understood it, and I said that, of course, the bills for goods supplied were posted in that column, and the cash paid posted in that column, and the other column showed if the account was in debit or credit, and there ought to be a cash book where the cheques that came in each morning were entered on one page, and the payments of those cheques into the bank were entered on the opposite page. If the old balance at the bank were entered at the top of the credits page, and the total of the new credits added underneath, I told them kindly, the figures underneath should be the new balance at the Bank. They gazed at me as if I were the Infant Samuel, and Mr Edwin said solemnly did I really think I could keep The Books? I gazed back soulfully, and said if Mr Burroughs would explain them to me I thought I could learn. The Accountant took off his pince-nez and wiped them, and he went as red as a beetroot and his chins quivered, and he said he would be delighted to try, so that was that. The poor young man wanted to join the Army, hence my promotion. I actually had a rise, though I don't remember how much, half a crown a week, I expect. Employers thought in half crowns in those days. The joy in being out of the general office under Doff's jurisdiction and in an office of my own, with ACCOUNTANT on the door, was honestly almost more than I could bear.

262

Mr Burrows spent one week painstakingly explaining the system of bookkeeping to me, and it was very straightforward. There were six or eight colossal great ledgers bound in boards with calf backs and arranged alphabetically, with gold letters on the backs. They went back nearly to the year dot I should think — they were the trade accounts, and a set of smaller ones, but not all that small, containing the Religious Society accounts, where we entered the donations that came in, and the cost of the advertisements, and the cheque paid over once a month for the balance — if any — after we had also deducted our 10% commission. We were scrupulously honest, of course. We just had one or two favourites among the people who had more money to spare for advertising. One more week the Accountant spent popping in and out — I think he was at a bit of a loose end — and generally seemed to be around at lunchtime, so we three went along to our everyday JP, and we introduced him to our twopenny steak puddings. He was a most solemn young man, with weak sight and very bad acne, and was much too plump and had wattles like a turkey cock, and a most embarrassing habit of blushing. He and Doff had worked in adjacent offices for quite a while and hardly exchanged a word, but after he went into the Army they corresponded regularly, until he was in one of the big pushes and was just blown to pieces. We had three young men from the office who were in the Army, Mr Herbert's son, Mr White, the handsome advertising manager, and young Mr Burrows, and all three were blotted out — that is what it was like in that horrible war. The sorrowing relatives so often just had no idea what had happened to their men, no body, no decent burial, just a number of bits disintegrating in the atmosphere, somewhere in France.

Doff was able to take on one of her Sunday School class girls as office junior, and if she had searched around for months I don't think she could have found a plainer one. She had very, very weak sight, and wore glasses with just about the thickest pebble lenses I have ever seen, and in addition, it really did seem too bad, she had the worst stickiest-out teeth I have ever seen, as well. They pushed her top lip right up so that her mouth never closed properly, and her large, gleaming red gums were always extremely prominent. The boys in the Packaging Department called her "The Gargoyle".

There was an internal switchboard extension through to my room, with my own instrument, and I felt very grand when calls were put through to me. There was one more largish book, quite a mysterious one, with PRIVATE LEDGER in gold on the front. It had a thick brass clasp from cover to cover, like those I have seen on many family Bibles since, which clipped over a brass loop and was held in place by a thick little brass padlock, the key to which was on one end of the thick gold watch chain which was draped across Mr Edwin's ample paunch, and which sat in a little pocket on his side front. I managed this job quite well, without any trouble, and for the first time had constant contact with the partners, and a pretty stuffy, starchy lot they were. If Mr Edwin wanted to know anything about the

264

accounts he either spoke to me on the internal phone, or he had to come down and look at the books, but never, never did those old men speak to one about matters of general interest, or treat one as a person. It was as if, however well one did a job, the fact that one received payment for it — and pretty pitiful payment at that — put one in a different world. They, with their fat purple faces and wobbly double chins, had just the same kind of minds as Mrs Dawson at Weston Hall. Their own precious young families were the only young people that mattered. The world existed for them, and the teeming crowds of young folk doing their housework and their office work were entirely negligible. We might have been so many automatons or zombies. Not young humans.

The week I was in the Accounts Office with young Mr Burrows was rather fun. The first day or so he was rather stiff and shy but then he began to loosen up. He told me, incidentally, that he was only joining up because he couldn't bear to sit in that office by himself any longer, his only contacts being those stodgy old men upstairs. I said why didn't he come into the general office occasionally, and talk to Doff and me and nice Miss Bell, but he went fiery red and said oh, he couldn't! But I had a glimpse of one of the ways prosperous businessmen made extra money. This young man's father had paid quite a sum of money to Mr Edwin, and he was supposed to be "Articled" to him, to learn to be an accountant, but all he did was to be immersed all day long in those wretched ledgers by himself, and attending evening school in the evenings,

265

and they paid him a miserable pittance that was no more than pocket money. He had quite a good sense of fun and enjoyed my cartoons of the old gentlemen, and even had a go at it himself. Quite lurid, some of them were.

There was no furniture in the office as such, but a high, wide desk was built in from wall to wall, filling about a third of the space, and there were two or three high stools, most uncomfortable, which one sat upon to work. The Ledgers stood up on end at each end of the desk with their edges touching the wall, which was of dark brown wood for at least two thirds of its height, and glass opaque with dirt to the grimy ceiling. The sole ornament was a calendar with large black and red figures, and over everything, including the calendar, was ink, several hundred years' worth, I should think, for there was black, green, red and almost grubby-looking purple all mixed together in the surface of the wood, making quite a thick encrustation, especially where it encountered ancient blobs of sealing wax and, incredible as it may seem, candle grease. I had visions of generations of clerks loading their quill pens as heavily as possible from the sunken inkwells and seeing who could throw their blots the furthest. I was fortunate for I had this passion for drawing, and had never, in my life, been allowed to indulge it, so I would work, really hard say, all the morning, and then, when the old gentlemen went home at about three o'clock, would spend most of the rest of the day with a pencil or a piece of charcoal.

266

Mr Ebling discovered quite early in my accountancy days from odd bits of paper, about this love of mine, and was most helpful and encouraging. He supplied me with pencils of varying softness or hardness, and the charcoal, but most wonderful, large sheets of white packaging paper, which had quite a good surface. And he searched around among the thousands of books on his shelves — some of which had not been moved for years, probably — and brought me books with reproduced black and white pictures of villages and scenes and people in Africa. They were mostly missionary books, of course. I also copied any photographs or copies of pictures of people from the art galleries that he or anyone else could get hold of. And I don't think I tore many up — always someone seemed to want them. Of course, while my drawing sessions were on, the desk in front of me was well screened with ledgers, just in case Doff decided to come in, though it was never very likely. All along the front of the desk were long, deep drawers, smelling rather of mice, and these were good hiding and storing places, too. I was pretty good at catching likenesses, and managed quite a passable one of Miss Bell and of Miss Holyoake too.

We were getting on now to the late autumn of 1915, and as I remember it, there was a heavy depression and gloom over London. I found afterwards that it was not so in the country districts. There was no rationing of food and goods, of course, and we were able to buy our whole leg of lamb every Saturday, but I think a lot of men lost their jobs or had to accept lower pay. I did not know the general position but only as it affected the families of the little girls I taught in Sunday School, but one family in particular I remember, of four little girls. Two of them were in my class. They were Welsh, very Welsh, and the father had come to London seeking work. He was a very highly skilled carpenter and wood-worker, but his skill was not needed in the second year of the war. No houses were being built, nor fine repairs done, and he was in the position of having to take the most menial jobs offered. He would tramp the streets for two days for a few hours work, wearing out his shoes, as his wife said. She did fine sewing, in her home, for some firm or other, but received very little pay for it. Several times, Blodwen, the nine-year old, dragged me round to "see Mam" and she proudly made me welcome, but I had a feeling both she and her husband were wearing themselves to the bone. They both had such a fine-drawn look, as though they could take just a very little more, and then would snap. She apologised for their two rooms, painfully bare and empty, but as clean as the proverbial new pin, saying "You couldn't get a house in London, as you could in Wales," but knowing what extreme poverty was — but not poverty as proudly borne as theirs — I wished so much I could do something to help them, but could do nothing.

In July, when Duncan was nineteen, he applied to the office for permission to join up — at that time Civil Servants were exempted — but it was refused so I still had him, and now, with our competent char lady, I had not too much to do in the evenings, and as he left work

268

at four, and I left at six, mostly he was outside the office waiting for me, having walked from Millbank, and we would have a pot of tea at JP, and a cream bun too, if we felt affluent, and then walk home to Highbury. I think the shops were lighted, though not too brightly, and the street lamps gave us a dim light too. I am sure the pavements were nothing like so crowded as they are now along Upper Street, and the roads were almost empty. Communications were so different from the last war, and every day was filled with rumours, of victories we had won, which the next day were contradicted. For weeks and weeks we had those stupid rumours about train loads of Russian soldiers, fully armed, with snow on their boots, making their way down from the north to the south to attack the Germans in France, and each night we believed something wonderful would be announced the next morning, but it never was, only the long, long lists of the casualties in the papers.

Appendix
Additional material from Sylvia White, daughter-in-law

G.A. White was known as "Bobs" by her husband Duncan and others who knew her as a young woman. Like many women of her generation, she lost her name when she became a mother and as her husband and children called her "Mum", so eventually did I as her daughter-in-law. As such I call her in writing this addition to her moving and horrifying story. I am writing this because although she did not like me, I was the only person she confided in. She learned, painfully, that neither her husband, children nor sisters believed in "raking over the past" but her pain and deprivation left scars which periodically opened. This became acute in old age and it was then that I suggested she try writing down her memories. She did but it met with disapproval from her sister Doff and her own daughter.

What stand out are her innate gifts, her intelligence and a basic belief in herself which fuelled her driving ambition to achieve and to better herself. She continued to read avidly and developed monetary skills, which she used to great effect in the second half of her life. Together, she and Duncan shared a love of music and taught themselves to play instruments; he the violin and she the cello. They both worked at losing their regional accents to the point where there was never a single vowel to act as a give-away, but this left a pedantic preciseness which could jar. Duncan was equally intelligent, well-read and ambitious but could brook no competition, so when, having taught her to play chess, she looked like equalling him, he refused to play with her. They also shared a love of gardening but again, no one was allowed to be better or more knowledgeable than he.

When Duncan joined up in the 1914-1918 war he became an army clerk working on supplies for the Royal Engineers building the Military Canal at Hythe, in Kent. Mum decided she wanted to be near him and took a job in a bank in Deal. This was a happy period in her life when she was full of romance and idealism. However, eventually her marriage was to bring her further hardship and shame.

After the war, Duncan returned to work as a Civil Servant in London, working on sending supplies to Tristan da Cunha and she to working in a bank. They managed to get a mortgage, bought a plot of land in Woking and had their house of dreams built. Labour was cheap at this time, so they had their dining room furniture made to their specifications by a local craftsman. The garden was large and Duncan lost no time in stocking it and making it perfect. In 1922 Mum gave birth to a daughter, Mary, and five years later to a son, Jeremy. Life was easy because she had a daily maid. However with Duncan's fares to London and their outlay on the house and garden, their finances were over-stretched and they borrowed from Doff and Jessie's husbands.

Duncan ran the Social Club at work and won the Chess Championship Cup. He "borrowed" money from the Social Club fund, intending to put the money back before the auditors came. His brothers-in-law refused further loans and Duncan was humiliated and dismissed. He suffered a total breakdown and acute asthma attacks and was admitted to a mental hospital. The children, aged three and eight years, were sent up to Lincolnshire to be cared for by their great-aunt Maggie and great-uncles Tom and Bob. Their sister, Duncan's mother, had died of TB when Duncan and his brother were very young. The boy's father also lived with them. Auntie Maggie ran the local grocery from the front part of their substantial property, and Bob was the local butcher, working from ancillary buildings behind the house. Tom was the signalman on the local railway. All three remained single.

The house in Woking had to be sold to pay their debts but there was enough money to buy a cheaper property that was rented out. Mum returned to live with one of her sisters in Islington and found work in a bank near Victoria. She spoke of the awful cold, wet waits for buses at the end of the day.

In those days people believed that it was a mistake to upset children by explaining troubles to them, therefore the children did not know what they had done wrong to

273

be sent away and they never had a single letter or message from their parents. This traumatic separation had life-long effects on both children.

Mum scrimped and saved and Duncan was eventually discharged and Mum was angry that he made no effort to find work. There was no understanding on anyone's part that he must have been acutely depressed. Mum scoured the adverts and found a backstreet grocer's shop for sale in a North London suburb, with living accommodation above the shop. Jeremy described the shock of being brought back from Lincolnshire to be confronted by bare, wooden stairs.

Despite financial restraints the children were sent to a little private school. The shop was part of a shabby Victorian terrace, which served all the neighbours with their daily needs. Poverty was rife at this time and shoppers bought small amounts of food on a daily basis; "a penn'orth o' potherbs" bought a potato, a carrot and an onion or turnip.

The children were not allowed to socialise with the neighbours and were brought up to believe that they were more intelligent and gifted than anyone else. Indeed they were taught to despise all but the famous, which made social interaction a problem for them. They were gifted and were trained to be musicians, Mary learnt piano and Jeremy the violin. For a time the family played chamber music together, until the children outgrew their parents' ability. Both became gold medallists at the Guildhall School of Music and the son became leader of his section in the Covent Garden Orchestra.

274

The Second World War was to open doors for Mum. She and Mary were directed to work at Standard Telephones and Cables. This was work of national importance and meant they could not be called into the Services. Mum saved her earnings in her own name and was able to buy two of the dilapidated houses in their street. She had started on the property ladder. With rents coming in they were able to buy a nicer property for themselves and let the property above the shop.

Mother and daughter not only worked together but they both sang in the Alexandra choir. Later on Mum joined the BBC Choral Society and made the acquaintance of numerous musicians and conductors, through whom she was able to promote her son's orchestral work, until he grew to resent her interference.

I first met the Whites in 1945 having met Jeremy and Mary at the Guildhall School of Music where I was a Drama student. Mum had a curious defence when she was shy or uneasy; she smiled a fixed smile, screwed up her eyes and focussed above your head, thus avoiding eye contact. She had no idea that this ploy was embarrassing for the other person. The Whites were keen on competitive board and card games and prided themselves on doing difficult crosswords. I quickly found that providing a clue that had stumped them was not acceptable. I also found that their son's determination to marry me had to be kept a dead secret. In the end we became officially engaged and he announced it as he left the house so that there could be no response. Mum left me in no doubt that I could never be a good enough match for someone who was a poet and a musician. Matters were made worse when Mary fell in love with one of my brothers! They could not face telling the Whites and kept their marriage a secret for months, even though Mary was twenty-six! Such was the resistance to outsiders that we never became insiders!

In 1953 Mum became noticeably ill and was coping with terrible pain. One day when they were visiting us I found her doubled up with pain. When I questioned her she told me that the doctor had diagnosed haemorrhoids. I queried this and begged her to go back to the doctor. She did, and was eventually found to have advanced bowel cancer. She underwent surgery at the Royal Northern Hospital, in Holloway, a grim place at that time. She was terribly ill after extensive surgery and was to suffer after-effects for the rest of her life but the cancer was successfully removed.

Mum made more and more money and she and Duncan retired to New Romney and bought a car. The number of properties and investments grew and after Duncan's death Mum used to come and stay with us. With her son out at performances she was stuck with me in the evenings, hence my learning much family history and encouraging her to write it down. She had showed the poems she wrote to her son for years and she certainly had a sensitive eye and use of pen.

Sadly, in the 1940s Mum had been given barbiturates and "uppers and downers" to help her "nerves" and to help her to sleep with the result that she became addicted. It was only in her eighties when she was in a Home and had had several strokes that she no longer noticed their withdrawal. We visited her and she was gentle and sweetly smiling, the first time I had met the un-drugged her. We have a lovely photo of her being pushed in a wheelchair by our youngest son, looking serenely happy in a way that I had never known her.

Also available in ISIS Large Print:

Clouds on My Windows

May O'Brien

May O'Brien was 15 in 1947 when she started to work in Liberty Hall, the union headquarters that sat beside the River Liffey. She soon discovered that it was as gloomy a place inside as outside, and that the most heinous crime was to neglect the coal fires that battled to keep the chronic dampness at bay. But as this spirited young woman comes to terms with the job and with her varied assortment of colleagues, the atmosphere of her story lifts, instilling the book with warmth, humour and affection.

Life was a struggle for May and her family, and she was glad to be able to contribute financially; she was glad, too, to find that she was appreciated in work. After her first three months in the job, and as the book ends, she reflects that she's learnt a lot from her union colleagues since she entered Liberty Hall as an impressionable school leaver.

ISBN 0-7531-9318-3 (hb)
ISBN 0-7531-9319-1 (pb)

A Midhurst Lad

Ronald E. Boxall

Although poverty and illness marred his young life, the author's sense of mischief and humour shine through this charming childhood autobiography.

Born into the Boxall family in 1924, Ronald was brought up in Duck Lane, Midhurst,: at that time an address synonymous with hardship. It is the tale of "the average life of an average boy born of poor parents, who lived under slum conditions, yet dwelt in the centre of a tiny and pretty town set in a near paradise of pastoral and sylvan delights". Ronald tells his story with natural wit and clarity, sharing his memories of a bygone age.

ISBN 0-7531-9320-5 (hb)
ISBN 0-7531-9321-3 (pb)